Young Writers 2005

Playground Poets

Let your creativity flow...

ode

limerick   haiku

rhyme

Cheshire

Edited by Steve Twelvetree

 Young**Writers**

First published in Great Britain in 2005 by:
Young Writers
Remus House
Coltsfoot Drive
Peterborough
PE2 9JX
Telephone: 01733 890066
Website: www.youngwriters.co.uk

SB ISBN 1 84602 100 6

Foreword

Young Writers was established in 1991 and has been passionately devoted to the promotion of reading and writing in children and young adults ever since. The quest continues today. Young Writers remains as committed to the fostering of burgeoning poetic and literary talent as ever.

This year's Young Writers competition has proven as vibrant and dynamic as ever and we are delighted to present a showcase of the best poetry from across the UK. Each poem has been carefully selected from a wealth of *Playground Poets* entries before ultimately being published in this, our thirteenth primary school poetry series.

Once again, we have been supremely impressed by the overall high quality of the entries we have received. The imagination, energy and creativity which has gone into each young writer's entry made choosing the best poems a challenging and often difficult but ultimately hugely rewarding task - the general high standard of the work submitted amply vindicating this opportunity to bring their poetry to a larger appreciative audience.

We sincerely hope you are pleased with our final selection and that you will enjoy *Playground Poets Cheshire* for many years to come.

Contents

Charley Jayne Robson (9)	15
Kyle Hunt (8)	16
Arron Fox (10)	16
Sam Gething (7)	16
Danielle Cope (7)	17
Leanne Pickford (11)	17
Thomas Proctor (10)	17
Hannah Milnthorp (11)	18
Jamie Luke Hardman (9)	18
Jack McLellan (11)	19
Jennifer Cossey (11)	19
Ryan Andrew-Fox (10)	20
Hannah Costin (8)	20
Alysha Reilly (11)	21
Rebecca Large (7)	21
Jessica Large (9)	22
Callum Berry (10)	23

Cheadle RC Junior School

Olivia Mooney (11)	23
Dayna Ellison (9)	24
Molly O'Shea (8)	24
Rebecca Shiel (10)	25
Jessica Nixon (10)	25
Elizabeth Martin (9)	26
Lucy Cunningham (10)	26
Naomi Lees (10)	27
Michael Platt (9)	27
Robert Wragg (11)	28
Bethany Rae (9)	28
Grace Taylor (11)	29
Jenna Hurley (11)	29
Bernadette Courtney (11)	30
Rachael Tait (10)	31
Joe Bevan (7)	31
Connor O'Callaghan (10)	32
Hannah Golden (9)	32
Daniel Pearson (8)	33
Jack Lightfoot (9)	33
Aimee Newsome (10)	34
Nathan Albiston (7)	34

Ainsley Marchant (9)	57
David Sheard (7)	57
Anthony Lomax (11)	58
Lucy McDermott (11)	58
Corinne Hutton (8)	59
Kate McDermott (8)	59
Olivia Booth (10)	60
William Shiel (7)	60
Matthew Gunn	61
Daniel Knowles (11)	61
Sandra Madathilethu (10)	62
Conor Ryan (8)	62
Matthew Trainor (10)	63
Caitriona Dooley (7)	63
Cillian Golden (7)	64
Ryan Miskell (11)	64
Conor Young (11)	64
Hannah Jefferies (11)	65
Charlotte Boardman (11)	65
Alexandra Heywood (10)	65
Chris Thorpe (11)	66
Thomas Sokolyk (11)	66
Callum McAllister (11)	67
Mary Enright (9)	67
Jamie Taylor (10)	68
Vicky Newsome (7)	68
Emily Wagner (9)	69
Daniel Harrison (7)	69
Sam Gibbons (9)	70
Sam Theophanous (9)	71
Clementine Kellaway (10)	72
Katharine Roddy (10)	73
Robert Caldwell (7)	74
Samantha Hince (9)	74
Thomas Fagan (7)	75
Ellie Lavelle (8)	75
Clare White (10)	76
Sean Connolly (9)	76
Ben Platt (10)	77
Jordan Goddard (9)	77
Megan Downes (9)	78
Courtney Wright (9)	78

Hannah Clayton (8)	79
Tara Cox (8)	79
Thomas Patching (11)	80
Kyle Albiston (7)	80
Sophie Doyle (8)	80
James Robinson (7)	81
Daniel Beasley (7)	81
Anna Lightfoot (7)	81
Benjamin McAllister (8)	82
Conor Craven (7)	82
Thomas Donaghy (9)	83
Amy Pullar (7)	83
Megan Grady (10)	84
Isabelle Foley (7)	84
Elliot Clyne (9)	85
Hannah Entwistle (7)	85
Oliver Clyne (9)	86
Adam Swales (10)	86
Victoria Gorton (7)	87
Faith Parker (8)	87
Naomi Tan (8)	88
Lucas Martin (11)	88
Alex Charnock (7)	88

Golborne Primary School

Gavin Clements	89
Summer Jones (8)	89
Zoë Jones (10)	90
Katie Bilsbury (10)	90
Zoë Draisey (11)	90
Nicole Thompson (7)	91
Claire Anders (11)	91

Kingsley St John's CE Primary School

Laura Warburton (9)	91

St Matthew's CE Primary School, Stockport

Hannah Goldsby (11)	92

Warren Wood Primary School

Amber Shun-Shion (11)	93
Matthew Salt (10)	93
Olivia Yates (10)	94
Lucy Thomas (11)	94
Michael Lee (11)	95
Dean Normington (11)	95
Samantha Bewes (11)	96
Joe Robinson (11)	96
Eleanor Cunningham (10)	97
Hannah Roberts (11)	97
Jack Boswell (7)	98
Georgia Bartosz (10)	98
Jake Norris (7)	99
Jack Rae (10)	99
Ben Gardiner (7)	100
Lucy Stead (10)	100
Liam Thomas Cocks (7)	101
Samantha Willows (11)	101
Molly Foster (10)	102
Fallon Mathieson (11)	102
Bradley Cook (11)	103
Tom Carey (10)	103
Hannah Maxwell (7)	104
Scott Williams (11)	104
Owen Burslam (7)	105
Daniel Goodwin (10)	105
Dean Leadbeater (8)	106
Liam O'Brien (10)	106
Sophie Torkington (8)	107
Jackie Liu (10)	107
Emily Roberts (7)	108
Ian Baguley (10)	108
Lewis Mitchell (7)	109
Keira Amber Mistry (7)	110
Hannah McMurray (7)	111
Rachael Warrender (8)	112
Ellen Taylor (8)	113
Hannah Wilson (8)	114
Jack Thornbury (7)	115
Alice Hillen (8)	116

The Poems

My Sister Caitlin

She is very, very, very, very naughty,
My sister, she is three but she is scared of bees
And she pretends to climb trees
She loves snapping leaves
She loves dogs and rabbits
Her favourite rabbit was called Fudge
And she never holds a grudge
She loses her voice because of her big mouth
She is three and her birthday is on Christmas Eve
And she receives lots of cards
She loves nursery, she goes nearly full-time
But by the time she comes home she is exhausted
But my sister . . . I love her very much!

Cassie Cartwright (10)
Adswood Primary School

Holly's Lifetime Poem

When I was eight I went to London
I went with my mate Jennifer
I got really frightened at the night
I also got a big fright
I missed my mum and dad so much
I felt awfully sick
I took some gifts home
I bought my mum a comb
I was so, so glad to see my mum and dad
When I was seven I went to Spain
I was not happy because we went on a plane
I was happy when I got there
Every night I went to a café and ate all the food in sight.

Holly McMahon (9)
Adswood Primary School

About Me

I'm a very lucky girl, every day is full of laughter.
Mum and Dad take care of me,
And I have a lovely big sister.
I've always lived in Adswood,
And I love to go to school.
There's lots to learn and friends to play with too,
And there is lots of fun to have.

Elisha Carter (10)
Adswood Primary School

My Feelings

When I am in conflict in I feel like I am being bullied.
When I am muddled I feel like a word that's never been used ever.
When I am doubtful I feel like a pancake being tossed, never stopping.
When I am droopy I feel like a glass of milk being spilt.
When I am uncertain I feel like someone put me in a spaceship
with maths homework and algebra
When I am confused I feel like a cow in a field with no grass.
Can you guess what I am feeling?
Well, I am not telling you . . .

Rowan Saenz (9)
All Saints CE Primary School

Sleepy

I feel like I'm in my own world
Floating across the wildlife
Diving into the sea, playing with the fish
And storming out back into a warm orange sky
Following the birds across, in and out of the fluffy clouds.

Jessica Walker (10)
All Saints CE Primary School

My Made Up Unicorn
(Inspired by 'Portrait Of A Dragon' by Moira Andrew)

For his head I'd use a big chunk of cream-white snow.
For his body I'd use a bag with cotton wool as soft as mice inside.
For his hooves I'd use string as black as night wrapped around
a small tub.
For his tail I'd use whipped cream and cotton as soft as cats' fur.
For his horn I'd need a lolly with swirls as twisty as sheeps' fur
and more colours than a rainbow.

Sarah Green (9)
All Saints CE Primary School

Great Giddiness

When I'm giddy I feel all warm inside
And it makes me feel like something's going to happen
So I wait all day until the surprise comes.
Sometimes I get a tingly feeling in my chest and it tickles me,
That's what makes me jump up with joy.
The warmness inside warms me up and comforts me,
It flows in me like the sea setting on the bumpy, golden sand.
Giddy makes me playful and also happy.

Natalie Kinsey (9)
All Saints CE Primary School

The Unicorn
(Inspired by 'Portrait Of A Dragon' by Moira Andrew)

For his head I'd use a big, round snowy ball.
For his body I'd use a rough, bumpy ball of stones.
For his hooves I'd use a coconut shell.
For his tail I'd use a dressing gown cord.
And for his horn I'd need an ice cream cone coated with swirly cream.

Sophie Mayor (10)
All Saints CE Primary School

Happiness

Happiness . . .
Is the sound of the sea
As it brushes up against the rocks

Happiness . . .
Is the scent of raindrops
As they fall to the ground

Happiness . . .
Is the taste of chocolate
As it melts in my mouth

Happiness . . .
Is the sight of birds in the famous seven
As they drift into the sunset

Happiness . . .
Is the sound of babies gurgling
As they crawl on their hands and knees

Happiness . . .
Is when I go to bed at night
And dream my favourite dreams.

Georgia Hooton (9)
All Saints CE Primary School

Hero - Cinquain

He hoped
to catch up with
other swallows as he
glided through the freezing cold air
racing.

Eric Fitchett (8)
All Saints CE Primary School

If I Was Lonely

If I was lonely . . .
I would be marooned on a faraway island
No one would come within one hundred metres of me
And I would be in a dark chrysalis on my own.

If I was lonely . . .
People would hate me
And my life would be pure misery
It would feel as if my parents and family lived in a different country
I would not know why I was ever born.

If I was lonely . . .
It would feel as if I'm the only one left
My colours droop down as I see my friends
Or what I call friends disappear
I come back and no one is here
I hate my life.

If I was lonely . . .
I would see people laughing and wish I were them
I don't believe in myself people say that's why I am unhappy
But that's not true
I hate my life!

Hugh Collett (9)
All Saints CE Primary School

Magical Unicorn

(Inspired by 'Portrait Of A Unicorn' by Moira Andrew)

For his head I'd use a white rose bud.
For his body I'd use an egg shape.
For his hooves I'd use a little bridge shape.
For his tail I'd use a lot of fluff.
For his horn I'd use a magical ice cream cone.

Paul Owen (8)
All Saints CE Primary School

Little Blue Bobble Hat

Little Blue Bobble Hat taking Grandma's picnic,
Decided to stop and pick some flowers,
Fell head first over a stick,
The picnic, just look the wolf devours.

'Where are you going?' he says.
'To my grandma's house.'
'OK, have a nice day.'
On her way she saw a mouse.

Skipping up to the house,
Opened the front door,
Tripped over a mouse,
And there she saw . . .

The wolf from in the wood,
Sat there as bold as could be,
Asked her if she could,
Be his breakfast or tea.

She started to speak,
And the wolf ate her,
Suddenly the wolf fell asleep,
Snoring loudly, urgh!

Jessica King (9)
All Saints CE Primary School

Hero The Brave Swallow - Cinquain

Gliding
through the air scared,
racing the dreadful wind,
dodging the strong hobby falcon
bravely.

Sophie Brennan (8)
All Saints CE Primary School

Little Red Riding Hood

Little Red Riding Hood
Made a picnic and went to see Grandma Jean.
She skipped through the wood
And saw a mean, green fighting machine.

The mean, green fighting machine
Saw Little Red Riding Hood,
She stopped and looked and leered
In the dark, gloomy wood.

'My, my,' said the mean, green fighting machine,
Little Red Riding Hood looked at the house,
'I bet you're off to see Grandma Jean?'
Squeak! went the mouse.

'Grandma Jean, your eyes are so big.'
'All the better to see you with.'
'And I especially don't like your wig.'
'All the better to let you live.'

Then the mean, green fighting machine
Made an attack for her.
Then her fantastic hero Hugh
Leaped out and saved her you see,
He smashed the window and chucked him through.

Rebecca Burney (10)
All Saints CE Primary School

Unicorn

(Inspired by 'Portrait Of A Dragon' by Moira Andrew)

For his head I'd use a white rose bud.
For his body I'd use a big tin painted white.
For his hooves I'd use a scrunched up newspaper with plastic
                                    on the bottom.
For his tail I'd use long strips of wool.
And for his horn I'd use a magic wand.

Rachel Moore (9)
All Saints CE Primary School

Loving Cats

Whiskers white and silky
Like a sweet ice finger.
Eyes shine back into yours
Like new shiny blue gold.
Paws pounce up happily
Like a soft, bright pink peach.
Coat is ginger and white
Like a gingerbread man.
Tail curled up in a ball
Like the sparkling moon.
Eyes gleam right back at yours
Like the shine of the sun.

Megan Tinning (9)
All Saints CE Primary School

Hero - Cinquain

Hero
Fluttering by
Diving into white clouds
Gives a silly look at himself
Hero.

Jimmy Lei (9)
All Saints CE Primary School

Hero - Cinquain

Hero
darting quickly
over the green mountains
with all the rest of the swallows
weaving.

Nathan Brennan (10)
All Saints CE Primary School

My Painted Unicorn

(Inspired by 'Portrait Of A Dragon' by Moira Andrew)

For his head I would use a snowy-white rose bud with dancing petals.
For his body I would use a chunk of silvery-white snow.
For his hooves I would use a piece of floating black silk.
For his tail I would use a strip of clouds drifting away.
And for his horn I would need a pretty fairy in a white dress
giving pretty dreams to children.

Amelia Cooper (8)
All Saints CE Primary School

Nature's Unicorn

(Inspired by 'Portrait Of A Dragon' by Moira Andrew)

For his head I'd use a crisp snow-white rose.
For his body I'd use a flock of woolly sheep in a big circle.
For his hooves I'd use a smooth tree stump with lots of bark.
For his tail I'd use a flowing tidal wave.
And for his horn I'd use a magical icicle twinkling in the sunlight.

Fred Keyte (9)
All Saints CE Primary School

Surrounded By Cats!

Tabby cats, slinky cats,
Big, white fluffy cats,
Massive cats, little cats,
I like all types of cats,
Cats are cute, cats are fine,
I love cats especially mine.

Jessica Dhaliwal (9)
All Saints CE Primary School

Sammy The Cat

Sammy moves gracefully,
Wide eyed, his tail curled up,
Cautious of the new place,
He twists beautifully.

The grass begins to sway,
Quickly Sam's ears prick up,
Looking out for danger,
He swiftly gets away.

The unfortunate mouse
Is pounced on by Sammy,
It was very lucky,
It got into the house.

Daniel Curtis (9)
All Saints CE Primary School

My Cat

Tail like a radar
Ears pointy like a knife
Whiskers shooting out like soft, shiny cotton wool
Sharp, curled up claws clutching to the rough red carpet
Looking proud of himself
Arches his ginger back
Eyes staring like the moon
Purring like an engine
And now sleeping like a baby, cosy and warm.

James Humphries (9)
All Saints CE Primary School

Playground Games

Some pretty girls play kiss chase,
Other crazy girls will have a race,
In high heels they run,
Just for fun.
Some boys play football,
With Ali for he is tall,
Other boys play tiggy off the ground,
Clumsy children trip up and hit the floor with a pound.
The normal boys who play football,
Very often fall,
Me and my girl group,
We all walk round in a troop.
All of us exchange some eyeshadow,
And we all take in the flow,
We always gossip,
And one of my friends can do a flip,
This all happens in one play,
'I enjoyed that break!' I say.

Jade Gallagher (11)
Dane Bank Primary School

I Was Walking In The Playground

I was walking in the playground
When I heard some noise.
I was walking in the playground
When I saw some boys.
I said, 'Hey you over there, let me play?'
'No Chloe Crooks,' and they walked away.
'Hey you over there, what's wrong with that?'
'No Chloe Crooks and that is that.'
The bell rang and we went inside,
I said to my teacher that the boys are telling lies.

Chloe Darlington Crooks (9)
Dane Bank Primary School

Time For Play

Some shy girls are skipping,
Others are whipping,
Some noisy girls are singing,
Some are thinking.

Some lively boys are talking,
Others are walking,
Some smart boys are running fast,
Others are running last.

Some fast children in races,
Others are doing their laces,
Children are screaming,
Others are daydreaming.

The bell is ringing,
People are still singing,
Others are silent like a pin,
Too late, time to go in.

Enma Cossey (11)
Dane Bank Primary School

Playground

When the school bell rings out
All the children scream and shout
They rush to the door
To the playground they adore
Children playing football on the ground
Naughty children messing around
Little children playing games
Bullies go round and call them names
Playtime is over
They all go back to class
To do that boring subject
It's called *maths!*

Robert Street (10)
Dane Bank Primary School

In The Playground

The bell goes,
The children excitedly run outside,
All you can hear is people having fun,
Near the end you hear a little cry,
The children shout, 'Tig, you're it!'
Or, 'I've scored a goal.'
I see children happy,
Not a sad face in sight.
I hear people laughing and joking around,
I do not hear a sad voice,
Not even a sad sound.
Sometimes I hear people shouting, 'Come here!'
Children are joyful,
Children try not to be sad.
I hear people shouting, 'I'm sorry, come here!'
But when the bell rings,
It's time to enter the class.
I see sad faces all around,
But tomorrow I might see those happy, little faces smiling at me.

Aimee Jenner (9)
Dane Bank Primary School

Play In The Playground

The bell rings for 12 o'clock.
I can hear loud children shouting, 'Yeah, let's play.'
I can feel the silent, cold wind,
I can hear boys shouting, 'Yeah, I scored a goal.'
I am kicking a rock-hard ball,
I am hearing builders building flats,
I can see green gates at the end of the playground,
I can hear boys and girls shouting, 'Hey, you're it!'
I see grass which belongs to our school fields.
I wish it was summer so we could play on the grass.

Joseph Nuttall (9)
Dane Bank Primary School

Playground

I can hear loud children shouting hooray!
I can hear Mary telling Harry to get off the grass.
Suddenly I can hear crying, Amy Regan has fallen over.
The playground is full of puddles,
Kay is so wet.
Abigail comes over and asks if I want to play on the poles.
Michelle blows her whistle,
She shouts, 'All packed lunches.'
But we still have to wait,
So Shamim brings a picture of Busted
Then it was our turn to have our dinner at last.

Leonnie Bradshaw (10)
Dane Bank Primary School

Bell's Gone

Loud children running out like bulls
Some are dashing round the playground
Grumpy teachers standing in the rain
Sad children crying because they're hurt
Some are sprinting for the football
Strict teachers telling off the kids
Chatty children talking to their friends
Some are screaming because they're hurt
Annoyed teachers drinking a cup of coffee
Hungry seagulls swooping down for some food
Some are eating children's crisps
Then the bell rings, everybody in.

Andrew Cook (10)
Dane Bank Primary School

In The Playground

I heard the bell,
Everyone in the school charged outside.
In the playground
I heard children shouting and laughing,
Teachers shouting at tall children,
Some children are playing tig,
Chloe, Liam and Sam were playing tiggy ramp
And Liam was it.
Elliot and Sol were playing football with Year Six,
They were winning 6-5.
When the bell rang we snuck inside.
We were upset that playtime was over.

Kane Hirons (8)
Dane Bank Primary School

The Bell Rang!

The bell rang,
Bad boys pushing hard,
Happy girls laughing excitedly,
Bossy teachers shouting loudly,
Grace fighting,
Megan hiding,
I'm crying because I got hit by the ball,
Chloe chatting to Nicole,
Conner's tooth fell out.
The bell rang again.
We all rushed in.

Charley Jayne Robson (9)
Dane Bank Primary School

At Playtime

One sunny morning at playtime,
I could see Andre, Joe, Jordan and Simon playing.
When the bell went I had to go into the classroom.
I had to do a test
Because I was off on Monday.
I had flu.
At dinner I saw some boys playing tig.
I heard some birds singing.
I was happy when I had to go in.

Kyle Hunt (8)
Dane Bank Primary School

At Break Time

At break time it is icy
And the children are slipping all over,
Like a sliding ant
And crying like a baby.
Suddenly the sun comes out,
It melts the ice before your eyes
And they try to slide but there is no ice,
They fall over like rocks tumbling down.

Arron Fox (10)
Dane Bank Primary School

In The Playground

In the playground I see kind children playing,
In the playground I see litter flying,
In the playground I see fast children racing,
In the playground I see children being giddy,
In the playground I see people playing football,
Then the bell rings,
We all rush back to class so we won't be late.

Sam Gething (7)
Dane Bank Primary School

The Feelings In The Playground

I am in the class and the bell goes,
I dash to the cloakroom.
The children leave, running to the playground.
Wanting to get there first.
Someone feeling miserable being left out,
Someone feeling jolly playing lots of games,
The bell goes and it's time to go in,
With children feeling a bit sad to go in.

Danielle Cope (7)
Dane Bank Primary School

At Break

Crazy children are running everywhere
like chimpanzees in a zoo.

Laughing children
are chasing each other.

Angry teachers getting cold and annoyed
with children not doing as they are told.

When the bell goes everyone is miserable
as we go in class, for another boring lesson.

Leanne Pickford (11)
Dane Bank Primary School

Playground Games

The bell rings for playtime.
I jump up with joy.
We run out and play football
But when the bell rings we make our way in.
I can't wait until home time
And as the bell rings again
I am as cheerful as can be.

Thomas Proctor (10)
Dane Bank Primary School

Loudness In The Playground

In the playground lots of children are screaming,
The bossy dinner lady is shouting and putting naughty children
against the wall,
But one unhappy child is crying.
She says she hasn't got anyone to play with
But when the extremely nice dinner lady talks to her
She goes off and plays nicely.
After break is over.
The seagulls come down
Like falling leaves off a tree
And eat curly, crunchy crisps
That have been dropped in the playground!

Hannah Milnthorp (11)
Dane Bank Primary School

Playground

That's the bell to have great fun,
I can hear everyone rush to the playground,
I hear the boys pick the football teams,
I can hear the cheer when Year 5 wins,
I hear all the team shout, 'Pass to me!'
My team feels happy when we're in the lead,
My friend Philip says, 'I'm never on Matt's team.'
Shamin and Leonnie always fall out,
Aimee moans that she's not on,
Jade chooses who to play with,
Aaron laughs at Daniel.
All in the playground.

Jamie Luke Hardman (9)
Dane Bank Primary School

The Playground

Noisy girls and strong boys stampede outside.
Skilful boys playing football, Year 6 win zero to nine.

Ear-splitting girls screaming so hard it hurts your ears,
Joyful boys playing hide-and-seek.

Happy children playing tiggy grid,
Happy children playing normal tig.

School children crying,
Bored children sighing.

Cheerless children wailing,
Unhappy children moaning.

Quiet girls and quiet boys walking inside,
Children groaning as the bell rings.

Jack McLellan (11)
Dane Bank Primary School

The Dane Bank Playground

All the children coming out from boring lessons,
Screaming, shouting, moaning and crying,
Playing tig, football and hopscotch,
A clumsy boy falls over playing tiggy scarecrow,
All blood on his knee, ouch!
Year 3 girls skipping, smelly boys running fiercely,
A small girl is sulking
Because she got caught in a game of tig.
Playtime is nearly over now,
The bell is going to *rrrriiiinnnnggg!*

Jennifer Cossey (11)
Dane Bank Primary School

On The Playground

Playing out on the playground,
What can I do?
I know, let's play football.
Playing out on the playground,
What can I do?
What can I see?
I can see hungry children eating food,
Dropping food on the floor.
The massive seagulls fly as quickly as rockets,
Eating toast and crisps like tigers,
Then flying back into the air,
Then the bell rings and everyone goes in.

Ryan Andrew-Fox (10)
Dane Bank Primary School

Playground

I love to play on a cold winter's day,
Where happy children run outside to the playground.
I can hear children shouting, 'I want to play tig!'
Bossy dinner ladies shouting, 'Play nice you two
Or else you will be in big trouble!'
I can hear the trees rustling in the breeze.
The bell rings, children slouch back inside
And everybody goes home happy
At the end of such a wonderful day.

Hannah Costin (8)
Dane Bank Primary School

Fun Outside

5, 4, 3, 2, 1 *ring, ring!*
Everyone rushing out of class,
Like a herd of rhinos charging,
Year 6 girls chatting, laughing, giggling,
Small boys racing, shouting, fighting,
Everyone's having fun outside,
Playing football, skipping or tig,
No one knows how long they've got
'Til they have to work again,
They're still playing, then everything goes quiet,
The bell has gone,
They all go in like mice,
But they all can't wait,
For the next playtime to begin.

Alysha Reilly (11)
Dane Bank Primary School

I Like It In The Playground

I like to play on a hot sunny day
When the happy children are excited.
I can hear children chattering in the playground.
It is nice to play and have fun all day
In the happy, happy playground.
The dinner ladies call,
'Don't be nasty you lot else you will go on the wall.'
The bell rings loudly in our ears for us to go in.
The happy children turn sad because they like playing
But in the end they go into class.

Rebecca Large (7)
Dane Bank Primary School

Playground Poem

We've just finished English,
Then the bell rings,
Can't wait to get outside to play.
Excited children running outside,
After five minutes most of the games have taken place,
Suddenly, 'Come here, right now!'
Someone is in trouble.
I wonder what they have done?
A boy is walking to the dinner lady with a puzzled face.
We carry on playing our game of tig,
Hearing footsteps one after another
Getting quicker and quicker.
'You're on now.'
'Can't get me.'
'You're on.'

It starts raining,
We all get called inside
And everyone is playing games and colouring pretty pictures.
Then it stops raining,
Yes we can play again,
Only ten minutes left.
It's all normal again,
Riinngg!
Bye for now,
Class time.

Jessica Large (9)
Dane Bank Primary School

Playground

People screaming and yelling
When the bell rang.
Getting their big or small coats,
Then they're playing fun games,
Boring games.
Year 6 or Year 5 playing football
Girls playing skipping.
I can smell hot dinners
And people going for their packed lunches
Then the bell rings.

Callum Berry (10)
Dane Bank Primary School

A Horse And The Sea

A horse is free,
Like the sea,
It can be lonely and sad,
It can be happy and glad.

A wave is like a horse charging,
Even in the distance you can see it largening,
A cloud of foam is what it leaves behind,
But sometimes destruction it can be selfish and unkind.

But don't be scared, don't run away,
I won't always leave you in dismay,
As I trot towards the bay,
I can hear people say,
'What a lovely view it is today!'

Olivia Mooney (11)
Cheadle RC Junior School

I Wish

I wish I was a popular girl
And wore a chain of diamonds and pearl.
I wish my hair had layers and was straight,
I also wish I could stay up late.

I wish I had a little smile,
At least for a little while.
I wish I had a king-size bed
And wore a crown upon my head.

I wish I had a posh Rolls Royce
And a pop star singing voice,
But I am Dayna, that's just me
And I'm as happy as can be.

Dayna Ellison (9)
Cheadle RC Junior School

Animals

Animals, animals, animals,
Happy as can be.

Big animals, little animals,
It's the animals we love to see.

They can fly, they can run, they can hop,
Just as they never want to stop.

Wild animals living in the jungle,
Tame animals living in a home.

The proud golden eagle,
The cuddly koala bear,
The fierce, stripy tiger,
Which one do you prefer?

Molly O'Shea (8)
Cheadle RC Junior School

Dog Kennings

Fast walker,
Noisy talker,
Quiet napper,
Nasty snapper,
Food eater,
Basket neater,
Rabbit chaser,
Fast racer,
Face licker,
Mud digger,
Good swimmer,
Fab winner,
Good pet,
Very wet!

Rebecca Shiel (10)
Cheadle RC Junior School

12 Facts About Little Brothers!

They are . . .
Sister-punchers,
Home-wreckers,
Mum-annoyers,
Bad-dressers,
Bed-wetters,
Smelly-bellies,
Bad-cleaners,
Loud-shouters,
CD-breakers,
Messy-eaters,
Nose-pickers,
Sugar-lovers!

Jessica Nixon (10)
Cheadle RC Junior School

I'm Just A Little Barn Owl

I'm just a little barn owl
And I'm trying to fly,
I sigh as my older brothers and sisters
Flap their golden wings in the sky.

I'm just a little barn owl
And I can't search for food,
Mummy and Daddy say I'm too young,
So I'm off in my sulking mood!

I'm just a little barn owl,
Cosy in my house,
Though I don't like it where we live,
Because there's no tasty rat or mouse.

I'm just a little barn owl
And I think day is too light,
That's why I'm not very fond of it
And terribly terrified of the night.

I'm just a little barn owl,
I've got a long way to go,
Before I turn into a grown up,
There's a lot more things I need to know!

Elizabeth Martin (9)
Cheadle RC Junior School

My Cat Kennings

Rat catcher,
Bird snatcher,
Ball chaser,
Fence climber,
Fight starter,
Messy eater,
Big sleeper,
Dustbin rooter.
My cat!

Lucy Cunningham (10)
Cheadle RC Junior School

Misunderstood

I am an owl, I can be timid at times
And I can be a powerful killing machine.
Some people may see me as an animal to watch out for,
Maybe because they think I could harm them.
No, I eat mice, voles, that sort of thing
That isn't brutal, it's nature.

I'm a wild animal and I should stay a wild animal
I don't thank humans that mistreat me
And think I'm a pet because I'm not.
Owls are built for the wild
If you want a pet, try a dog.

I had a home, yep, a cosy little barn
That barn was a part of me:
My mind and my feathers.
I loved it so but now all that remains
Is a pile of rubble in a skip.

A whole flock of owls disappeared last month
With a few loud bangs,
My mother was amongst those few.

Leave me and my species alone.
We're built to last so let us last.

Naomi Lees (10)
Cheadle RC Junior School

Puppy, Puppy!

Puppy, puppy I can't wait,
Until I choose you as my mate.
Puppy, puppy makes me proud,
Puppy, puppy be dead loud.
Yellow, black, brown or spots
I will love you lots and lots.

Michael Platt (9)
Cheadle RC Junior School

Killer Of The Skies

I am an owl,
One of the most powerful birds of prey,
I am no ordinary, wise, fairy tale creature,
I am much more!

I am a ruthless killing machine,
I can feel the heartbeat of my prey,
Where they are and what they are doing,
Then when the time is right I swoop down, swiftly and silently,
Putting my dagger-like feathers through the air for the kill.
Thrusting my claws into my helpless victim,
Then flying back home silently to feed my family.

I can't be hunted and I'm hard to kill,
Even humans find me hard to kill.
I am like a panther, silent and vicious,
But I consider myself more powerful.

So next time you leave your home you'd better watch out
Because next time it could be you . . .

Robert Wragg (11)
Cheadle RC Junior School

My Cat

My cat has a teddy that wears a hat
and he sits on a mat. Fancy that?
He goes out all night but he never fights.
He comes home in the morning
and never stops yawning.
He sleeps on the couch,
he's a bit of a grouch.
That is why he is so fat,
oh my lovely white, furry cat.

Bethany Rae (9)
Cheadle RC Junior School

Misunderstood

I'm not that wise and I'm not that old,
There's a different story to be told,
I'm vicious, ferocious, lean and mean,
At night-time only am I seen.

My razor-sharp claws,
My ripping jaws,
My eyes jet-black,
My feathers muddy brown,
This is me as I swoop down town.

My wings spread wide,
I glide down low,
My prey has no chance, it's mine for tea
And then I take it home with me.

This is the real me,
Not fluffy or cuddly as you can see,
So now you know you've got me wrong
Totally misunderstood.

Grace Taylor (11)
Cheadle RC Junior School

A Lot Of Fear

Screaming noises in my head,
Tease and taunt me in my bed,
Fear is clear across my face,
Like a ghost in a haunted race,
Terrifying and scary.

Shadows on my bedroom wall,
A dozen ghosts at a ball,
How to take all these fears away
Go to Mum she'll tell me it's OK.

Jenna Hurley (11)
Cheadle RC Junior School

Feelings Of Loneliness

I once had best friends
That's all changed now
They ignore me
They do not care if I am upset
I have other friends
But none of them are my best friends
I am a reject not wanted
All I want is someone kind
Someone who will like me
Not a liar, a troublemaker
I have been forgotten
No one cares about me
You can't always trust your friends
They might turn into your enemies
I do not want to be a loner
I want to be in a group, a gang, a club
Or have my old best friends back
But no, that will not happen
They hate me, I do not hate them
Can't we go back to normal?
I wish we could
But we can't, never ever
What happened? Nothing.
No fight, no argument, just no friend
2 friends, 1 friend
No friends, a loner.

Bernadette Courtney (11)
Cheadle RC Junior School

First Day

The playground is jam packed
I try to find my way around
There are too many people
And have lost the school map

Everyone is so big
I'm so little
They all have friends
I can't find mine

One minute I'm the top of the school
Next minute I'm the youngest
Everyone used to look up to me
But now I look up to them

I have finally spotted my best friend
I'm running towards her
At last I found someone I know
Now I don't feel as scared!

Rachael Tait (10)
Cheadle RC Junior School

My Teeth And Me

My teeth, my teeth are shiny
My teeth are clean
When I go to the dentist he says, 'Great!'
When I look in the mirror they sparkle like stars.
My teeth are my friends, I am theirs too
I like going to the dentist, it is like my playtime
Others hate it, it's like their enemy
In the sun my teeth shine
My teeth shine
My teeth are clean!

Joe Bevan (7)
Cheadle RC Junior School

Sea Hawk

The sea is like a hunting hawk,
Soaring down behind his unwary prey,
Swamping the beach with a deafening squawk,
On a very stormy day.

When he has eaten his prey,
He glides home just as the waves retreat,
He is pleased at the end of a successful hunting day,
But he will return when the tide pounds upon the beach.

But on sunny summer days when the sea is calm,
The hawk glides high above the clouds,
He seems so small as if he could fit in your palm,
Neither sea nor hawk make any sounds.

Yet on bright spring days when the breeze is blowing,
The hawk races the wind, testing his speed,
The air is so cold you might think it should be snowing,
But to the strong gusts the hawk pays no heed.

Connor O'Callaghan (10)
Cheadle RC Junior School

The Shop

I go to the shop every day,
I always see my friend Clair and her teddy bear,
I go up to the till to pay my fee
And then I go home and have a cup of tea.

All my pocket money I spent today
And when my funny brother came I laughed away
And didn't know what to say
And that's my day!

Hannah Golden (9)
Cheadle RC Junior School

At The Beach

Orange fireball in the sky,
Shells scattered on the shore.
A flock of seagulls flying high,
The cold sea makes their bodies raw.

The tide has finally gone out,
Rock pools are in sight.
'Hurry,' comes the child's shout,
'Ow! That fish gave me such a bite.'

Waves crashing on the rocks,
Children playing with bucket and spade.
Mum is packing up the coolbox,
There remain the sandcastles that we made.

Sun setting in the sky,
Sandy bodies, sandy feet.
Time to go, say goodbye,
A day of fun, a smashing treat!

Daniel Pearson (8)
Cheadle RC Junior School

Spring

As the buds start to sprout,
The hens start to shout,
Off come the sheep's winter coats,
As boats start sailing on the moats.

The farmers gather their crops
And send them to the shops,
Then they're off to go abroad,
To places poor people can't afford.

As the snow begins to shift,
People's spirits appear to lift,
As the gloom gives way to light,
The day eats into night.

Jack Lightfoot (9)
Cheadle RC Junior School

A Wise Old Thing

People think I'm a wise old thing
But they don't know my true side,
For I'm an extreme killing machine
No sound I make as I fly.

For I'm the most powerful around
I just concentrate and my food is found,
I use my binocular vision and my supersonic hearing
And I'm like a jet plane speeding
As I swoop down to catch my tea
All the animals are afraid of me

I'm always on the lookout you see,
No one can ever harm me
Even when I am asleep
My big round eyes can always peep.

So you try being me for a day
I doubt you'll think the same about birds of prey.

Aimee Newsome (10)
Cheadle RC Junior School

A Winter Poem

The snow was gently falling
Ice crystals fluttered to the ground
It all was quiet
I couldn't hear a sound

I went outside to have some fun
To have a big snowball fight
I threw a snowball and got my friend
Both of us soon were all white.

Nathan Albiston (7)
Cheadle RC Junior School

The Environment

Why is everyone so mean?
Why don't people care?
Why don't people like the colour green?
Why don't people like clean air?

I don't know, don't ask me,
I don't have one good reason why,
People can't see,
What they do as they go by.

Don't people have minds today?
Or can't they care less?
I bet if ducks could talk they would say,
'Why do you want to hurt me? I'm in such a mess'.

Don't drop your banana skin,
Or your orange peel,
Here's a message, I'd like you to spare a min
Let's make a deal . . .

Put your rubbish in the bin.

Samantha Rowland (11)
Cheadle RC Junior School

Dalmatian Poem

D almatians are spotty
A nd I'm Dalmatian potty!
L ovely and soft
M ine runs up to the loft
A lways making a mess
T hey never ever rest
I love them so much
A nd over the moon and through the bush!
N ever ever fear
S o many Dalmatians are here.

Laura Keaveney (8)
Cheadle RC Junior School

The Hoot Of The Owls

I am a barn owl
And a bird of prey,
My family all live in the wild
But I am stuck here in this cage.
I hate loud noises
And I hate my vision
You see I can see ten times better than you
But at a cost
My world is in black and white.

Now you see,
Not all of us owls are nocturnal,
It's easy you see
If we have orange eyes we are around at dawn and dusk
If we have yellow eyes we are around in the daytime
If we have dark eyes (then like me) we are nocturnal.

My feathers I believe are extremely unique
I have sharp claws,
Fantastic feathers,
Beautiful colours.
Wonderful wings,
Beady eyes
And I am such an elegant flyer
But all of us owls are misunderstood.

Some of you humans see us as killing machines
Just because we eat other animals,
But so do you
You eat other animals but also scare them out of their homes
You cut down trees.
Everyone sees me as the wise old owl
But that's not true
I don't wear glasses or read books
I'm just simply misunderstood.

Emma McClusky (11)
Cheadle RC Junior School

Tiger Hunt

In India a day begins,
The sky is shot with gold and pink,
Among the grasses,
There lies a tiger,
Relaxing without a worry,
There is a click of a gun,
The tiger is alert.
The gun is held by a hunter,
Aiming carefully,
Pull of a trigger,
The tiger's off!
Bounding for all it's worth,
Through the grasses,
To the trees.
But there is another bang,
The tiger falls!
Oh why couldn't they leave them alone?
A cheer goes up,
Photos are taken,
Triumphant voices speak,
The sky is red now,
Oh why is life so unfair?

Katrina Davies (9)
Cheadle RC Junior School

Sense

Anger is a black stick that snaps in the middle of happiness,
Happiness is a golden globe shining during darkness,
Hurt is an ear-piercing scream in the middle of silence,
Laughter is a smile after depressing times,
Fear is poison during long, happy days,
Relief is a mended, broken heart.

Niamh Maguire (10)
Cheadle RC Junior School

Kennings Sister

She's an . . .
Annoying-sister
Headache-maker
Cake-baker
Sweet-eater
Doll-player
Telly-watcher
Music-dancer
Jewellery-wearer
Fussy-feeder
Bossy-leader
Lolly-licker
Cringer-whinger

But she's a . . .
Great-smiler
Helpful-helper
Energetic-bouncer
Fast-grower
Hair-curler
Alright-singer
Cat-lover
Attention-seeker
Fair-sharer
Happy-clapper
Active-tippler
But in the end . . .
She's my special sister!

Thomas Flanagan (11)
Cheadle RC Junior School

At School

In the playground, in the playground,
The teachers stay away.
Children running all around,
It's a great time of the day.

At lunchtime, at lunchtime,
All of us are eating food.
My friend's drink is flavoured lime,
We are all still in a good mood.

In the classroom, in the classroom,
One of us turns on the light.
This class could be doom
And the teacher gave me a fright!

It's home time, it's home time,
The work I did was pretty poor,
But that's not really a crime,
The bell went and everyone ran out the door.

Robert Adams (10)
Cheadle RC Junior School

The Lady Of Shalott

The darkness fell which she did fear,
And the crying came tear by tear,
Her weeping was all anyone could hear,
As if through her heart there was a spear
And dark clouds blew over Camelot.

Then the light grew dark and began to wane,
Never would she come again,
Along that long and winding lane
The Lady of Shalott.

Rosie Halligan (9)
Cheadle RC Junior School

Sheepdog

The farmer gave the sheepdog a command
And upon the dog's head placed one hand
At once the dog was sprinting across the land
Determined to finish the farmer's demand

Jumping hedges, dodging bundles, ducking trees
Trying his best to please
He kept on running, stretching his knees
He could hear the bees

He started chasing the sheep
Through a grass heap
At times you could hear a peep
He put the sheep in the pen
Where they went to sleep.

Danielle Charters Christie (9)
Cheadle RC Junior School

Failed Parachute

Falling, falling deeper still,
All he could do was feel ill.
His hands were twisted like puppet strings,
He tossed into the blackness,
Still falling, falling.
Falling, falling towards the ground
Not sorry, no emotions to be found.
The sadness, the darkness, not a thing,
His body all left a-quiver,
Then a glitter and sparkle flew up in the air.
Just a few moments later
And he was gone.

Peter Feehily (10)
Cheadle RC Junior School

The Dolphin's Wishes

I am being hunted,
I am being hunted so I have to go to a zoo,
Why do I have to go to a zoo?

You pollute the sea,
I live in the sea,
Why do you pollute the sea?

I get caught up in the fishing nets
And it's not my fault,
Why do humans hunt living things?

I am being eaten by sharks,
I know I have to be eaten,
Why couldn't scientists keep the sharks
Away from the baby dolphins?

My friends and family,
All swept onto the beach,
Lost from our sight,
Why do you let it happen?

Nicole McMullan (10)
Cheadle RC Junior School

A Fistful Of Pacifists

A choir of footballers
An understanding of different languages
A healthy of hospitals
A miaow of dogs

A whisper of loudness
A speed of snails
A light of darkness
A coldness of fire.

Holly Saxon (10)
Cheadle RC Junior School

Sammy The Snake

Here comes Sammy slithering through the grass
Sliding slowly in order to finish his task
Here comes Sammy circling all the trees
Licking his lips at what he sees.

Here comes Sammy flicking his wet tongue
His smooth, slender body extremely long
The green scaly creature has given a bewildering stare
I now know that I must take great care.

Here comes Sammy gliding round and round
I'm standing still, not daring to make a sound
Here is Sammy snapping at my heels
There goes Sammy, how does his tummy feel?

Joseph Stiles (8)
Cheadle RC Junior School

Playtime

The bell goes, children charge out,
In the playground children scream and shout,
Some play football or some just chase,
Round and round they play and race.

A group of girls stand and chat,
Whilst others play with ball and bat,
Some play netball, pass and score,
But at the end the game's a draw.

Dring, dring! Oh not the end of play,
Not dreaded maths with Mrs Kay,
I've remembered it's PE today,
The bell has rung, it's the end of play.

Joshua Pearson (10)
Cheadle RC Junior School

The Killing Machine

I am a killing machine, a hunter of the night,
I hunt for food and for fun.
I glide through the night to seek my prey,
I see a mouse and come down strong
And I stab it with my talons.
So if you think I'm cute then think again,
If you come near me then all you will get is *snip-snap*,
Until you're dead.
So all you mice out there,
Be warned, as I have eyes of flames.
I am an Aston Martin, speeding on the road,
So keep away from me, or you'll regret it,
For I am the killer of all.

Tim Mayall (11)
Cheadle RC Junior School

Horrible Noises

The worst noise is a blackboard screech,
Or is it a scream on a dreadful beach?
I hate those horrible noises,
The worst noise is a chair scraping on the floor,
Or is it a stone scratched down a wooden door?
I hate those horrible noises,
The worst noise is a baby's scream,
Or is it someone getting sick on cream?
I hate those horrible noises,
The worst noise is your shoe screeching against the floor,
Or is someone spitting out an apple core?
I will never like any of these horrible noises.

Michael Caris (9)
Cheadle RC Junior School

The Real Owl

The owls in cartoons,
Confident and wise
Are not the real me
That's me, but in disguise

I hunt and catch my prey
To feed my family
But the food could be poisoned
And I can't cook a remedy

It's very lucky for me
Because I'm not locked up in a zoo
I've lost some of my family
My brother and my sister too

I am a bird of prey
And I know that when I die
My skin will be used,
Stuffed like the filling of a pie

So leave us alone
We don't like it, you see
I am a wild bird
That desperately wants to be free.

Emily Carr (11)
Cheadle RC Junior School

The Lady Of Shalott

Lancelot hears a cry of pain,
He knows his journey was not in vain,
He whips his horse and pulls its rein
And thunders to the cursed dame,
The Lady of Shalott.
He clambered up the stony wall
And then he heard a distant call,
He saved her and they had a ball,
On the road to Camelot.

Vicki Bellairs (9)
Cheadle RC Junior School

The Turtle's Troubles

I wish you didn't come
with your nets and traps
to catch me and my friends
and keep us as pets
to put us in captivity
to let people poke me and point at me
and make fun of us
and our speed on land.
But we are never as fast as you
and your fishing boats
and when you catch us
and use us as pets
you soon get fed up with us and we die
so please stop
leave us alone
to swim by ourselves on a hot, empty beach
and live in peace.

Christopher Hutchins (10)
Cheadle RC Junior School

My Night Kennings

Skin-crawler
Branch-faller

Hair-raiser
Star-blazer

Shadow-maker
Leaf-raker

Midnight-creeper
Silence-keeper.

Eleanor Jones (10)
Cheadle RC Junior School

The Sheep's Hopes

I may look like a ball of fluff to you.
But I'm more - much more!
I see you with your woolly jumpers
And then I remember
That was once my wool and I want it back!

When you come to the farm
And you feed my babies
I, the mother don't get an input in it!
If I had my way, you wouldn't be anywhere near them!
The problem is, my owners don't keep me safe
From wolves or anything!
And when they come to round us up
They use dogs to bite our legs!
My hope is for it to stop; right now!
To be safe from wolves, and not to be bitten by dogs!

And when you come to the farm,
Just remember I may look like a ball of fluff to you,
But I'm more - much more!

Christopher Johnson (10)
Cheadle RC Junior School

Laughter

Laughter is yellow like a beaming sun.
It looks like happy memories and your dreams come true.
It reminds me of great things that haven't happened yet.
It tastes like there's a party in my mouth and everyone's invited.
It smells like a fantastic birthday cake of mine.
It sounds like jolly people laughing.
Laughter, laughter, laughter, I love it.

Thomas Walters (11)
Cheadle RC Junior School

The Whale's Wonders!

I have many fears, in my water home, beneath the sea.
Your nets surround us and capture us,
Your boats leave pollution in our oceans.

I have so many sorrows, for my family dying,
You hunt me and other sea creatures,
I have hardly any food left because of you.
We are almost extinct.

You laugh at my absurd tail and fins,
You hunt me and you laugh at me,
All I want is to have a life.

To swim in peace in the ocean
And to have some respect from you.
I just want to live in clear, cool waters of the ocean.

Alisha Krystek (10)
Cheadle RC Junior School

Butterflies

There is a butterfly in the garden.
All different colours, pink, purple, blue and green.
It floats amongst the flowers and sometimes can't be seen
She looks so beautiful swaying her wings in the sky
Now she's flying way up high
Far away there is more
They might come flying at my door
I wish I was one
Oh no now she has gone
I hope it comes back one day
A bright and flowery day in May . . .

Anya Neill (7)
Cheadle RC Junior School

I Know Someone

I know someone who can balance the biggest mansion in the world,
On a short strand of hair,
Whilst driving a super sports car in the air.

I know someone who can play two games of Monopoly,
Whilst playing football against David Beckham and saving a goal,
With my favourite dolly.

I know someone who can eat Smarties with chopsticks,
Whilst reading the encyclopaedia and painting the Mona Lisa.

I know someone who can build a Tudor palace,
Whilst knitting and flying around the universe in a chariot.

I know someone who can operate on a patient,
Whilst wearing a straight jacket,
Their eyes closed from inside a sack.

I know someone who can look for a needle in a haystack,
Whilst eating sweetcorn with custard and cream,
All in one minute!

And that someone is me!

Hannah Robinson (11)
Cheadle RC Junior School

The Runaway

No one there to see me smile,
No one there, I'll wait a while,
No one there to tell me off,
No one there to cure my cough,
No one there to see me play,
No one there to see the sun's rays,
No one there to switch me on,
No one there, 'cause I've just gone.

Catherine Livesey (9)
Cheadle RC Junior School

The Deer's Fears

I am a stag.
I am a royal with twelve tines.
I am the leader of the herd.
I fear humans, the bringers of violence.
I scent something on the breeze.
A sickening stench fills my nostrils - the stench of humans.
I bellow and bolt, the whole herd follows my example.
The stench gets stronger and stronger.
I look back and to my horror, I see the herd is no longer following me
But the humans are.
The humans are riding on strange creatures.
Smaller and more vicious creatures run on ahead of them.
The humans are carrying black sticks and aiming them at me.
My heart is pounding violently against my chest.
My legs feel so heavy I can hardly lift them.
A thunderous noise echoes in the dark forest.
I feel a pain in the back of my neck.
One last cry escapes my lips and everything goes black.

Dara Roden (11)
Cheadle RC Junior School

The Monkey's Dream

I'm having a really bad day,
Just leave me alone and go away.

I'm stuck behind bars when I want to be free,
People keep pointing and laughing at me.

If I lived in the wild I'd explore all day long,
I'd climb the highest tree and hear the bird's song.

But I'm not, I'm stuck here feeling unhappy and sad,
Please go away, you're driving me mad.

Katy Pearson (11)
Cheadle RC Junior School

The Mobile

The police bought the flashy mobile
So he was cool.
Not like the guy down the street,
He really was a fool.

The mobile was very useful calling the police
To catch the crooks.
Not like the other mobile, all he did was
Sit and watch the ducks.

The mobile was a flip phone made of silver,
Yes indeed.
The mobile down the street
Looked more like seaweed.

The phone got bored of the police
Who as cool,
So it sold itself to the
Fool!

Alex Trimble (10)
Cheadle RC Junior School

Kennings Dog

Face-licker
Slipper-nicker
Cat-chaser
Mouse-hater
Quick-runner
My-stunner
Meat-eater
Lazy-sleeper
Ball-keeper
Great-leaper.

Jonathan Hall (11)
Cheadle RC Junior School

The Fox's Feelings

I have a mind full of feelings,
But I want to have a full stomach.
Let me be free of hunters, dogs and horses,
Don't make me be afraid!

I'm just a cartoon to all you humans,
Always the baddie, slinking around in stories
And making mischief!

Why do I have to be the one
Who everyone calls 'sly' and 'cunning'?
When I come into your back garden
Don't throw things at me!
I'm only looking for food!
Let me be wild and free
To feed my family!

Abbie Smith (11)
Cheadle RC Junior School

Dogs Kennings

Cat-chaser
Fast-pacer
Bone-eater
Fire-heater
Meat-tearer
Slipper-wearer
Bum-licker
Sausage-nicker
Poo-dropper
Bad-hopper
Puddle-maker
Morning-waker.

Conor Egan (10)
Cheadle RC Junior School

Girl Swimming

(Inspired by 'Boy Flying' by Leslie Norris)

Swimming,
She saw a plane like a flying boat
A dolphin leaping over the waves,
Shimmering tuna fish gliding through the crystal clear, blue sea.
> She could not see the teacher giving out the homework,
> The children freezing when the bell rings,
> Children getting disciplined by the teacher.

Swimming,
She felt the blazing hot sun,
She felt the rubber lilo,
She felt the slippery fish,
> She could not feel her smooth maths book,
> Her wooden pencil in her hand.

Swimming,
She heard the screeching of a seagull,
The waves crashing against the rocks,
The laughter of happy children.
> She could not hear the screeching of the chalk on
> the blackboard,
> Pencils on the paper
> And the school bell.

Francesca Barnwell (9)
Cheadle RC Junior School

Sparkling Night

Fireworks flying
Bursting into showers
Catherine wheels go round
Fireworks as pretty as flowers
Fireworks flying all around the place
Some with a mighty spark
They glitter and shine
And cover the park.

Sarah Miller (7)
Cheadle RC Junior School

Girl Swimming

(Inspired by 'Boy Flying' by Leslie Norris)

Swimming,
She saw a school of silver fish,
She saw the pebbles under her feet,
She caught a glimpse of a dolphin.
  She could not see homework or other people.

Swimming,
She felt the water around her,
She felt the sun beaming through the water,
She felt the rubbery skin of a dolphin.
  She could not feel her handwriting pen.

Swimming,
She could hear the cry of a dolphin,
She could hear the ripple of the water.
  She could not hear the traffic and people arguing.

Emilia Granelli (9)
Cheadle RC Junior School

The Monkey's Moan

I swing through the trees you planted,
I stare through an invisible wall,
Where my fat lazy cousin hides behind.
I want to live,
I want to smell.
Think about I, think of me, not yourself.
I'd like to see without being blinded,
By the flashing light,
To please the tourists
While you make money out of me
And my misery.

Joshua Noble (10)
Cheadle RC Junior School

Schoolboy Football

At half-past 12 the school bell rings,
All the boys pack up their things.

Down the corridor we all run,
We grab the ball it's going to be fun.

All the boys tackle and shout,
Get stuck in and run about.

I have a shot and nearly score,
The keeper saves it, I must try more.

The goalie kicks the ball out in the air,
One boy shouts, 'Quick over there.'

I win the ball, the game's not over yet,
I have a shot, it's in the back of the net.

Goal!

Thomas Millar (8)
Cheadle RC Junior School

My Poem Of The Sea

The sea is an army of ants,
Deadly soldier ants,
On the march,
Marching and marching,
Never-ending,
Destroying everyone on its route,
Like a terrible tsunami,
Sucking in more water,
Moving forward - as fast as a jet plane,
Faster and faster,
Destroying everything on its route!

Beathan Hopkins (10)
Cheadle RC Junior School

The Dog's Wishes

I lie here in my pen
Dreaming one day,
That my wishes will come true.
A happy home and a loving family.
Fields to run in,
Children to play with.
A ball to follow, a stick to chase.

In my dreams I lie in a basket in a warm place,
Chewing my bone by the fire.

I wake up, a family is looking at me.
They are talking about adopting me,
My wishes are coming true,
Hooray!

Rory Denny (11)
Cheadle RC Junior School

The Sea Is A Lion

The sea is a lion,
It roars like the waves,
His tail flicks around,
Like the kids splashing.

The lions yawn
Like a boat's fog horn
They love to run around,
Like waves splashing on the beach.

Then they sleep all quiet, so quiet
Like the peaceful sea, just smooth and calm.

Ashlene Kozij (10)
Cheadle RC Junior School

Christmas Day

I open my eyes, it's cold and dark in my room,
I draw back the curtains to see the snow slowly drifting down
Like twinkling stars falling from the sky.
I quickly pull on my dressing gown and slippers and run downstairs.
The Christmas tree stands to attention like a soldier,
I run to the back door in the kitchen and step outside,
Crunch, crunch, crunch, my footsteps on the white, crispy snow.
It's Christmas Day!
I run back inside to see my presents under the tree.
I skip upstairs. 'Mum, Dad, wake up, it's Christmas!' I shout.
They don't hear me, but I run back down the stairs
And happily open my presents as Mum and Dad come downstairs.

Olivia Coleman (11)
Cheadle RC Junior School

The Pheasant's Complaint

I am only seen as a roast dinner,
Nobody sees my personality or spirit,
Nobody notices my fine plumage,
All I want is to be loved,
Even my rich owner only buys me for the shooting day,
Poachers are cruel
And kill me for pleasure.
I am overfed and forced to be tame.
I am only seen as a roast dinner.
Please think of me and love me,
For who I am.

Siân Davies (10)
Cheadle RC Junior School

Woman In Blue

The woman in blue was born in June,
She was special, the woman in blue.
She was kind and loving,
The woman in blue.

The woman in blue got married,
She had a daughter, the woman in blue.
She called her Valerie,
The woman in blue.

The woman in blue became very ill,
She looked as dull as a pill,
But when the time came,
The woman in blue died in the colour she knew.

Ainsley Marchant (9)
Cheadle RC Junior School

Louis The Dog

My dog Louis is a toy spaniel
He's not very keen on my brother Daniel,
He's got a button nose and two floppy ears
And when he cries he has wet tears.
He tugs the socks from off your feet
He really likes a doggy treat,
My ears and nose he likes to nibble
And after that he has a piddle.
Every day he sits on my lap
Then he ends up having a nap.

Ah, peace at last!

David Sheard (7)
Cheadle RC Junior School

Playground Dare

The playground is a jungle, a wilderness of people,
Wherever I go, to the deepest ocean or the highest steeple,
The teachers follow me everywhere,
I will show them, and then they will care,
I must perform a playground dare.

I must travel into the lion's lair,
When I am there,
I shall perform my playground dare.

I shall take a pen,
And once I have counted to ten
And checked that there is no fear,
I shall change all school records to clear.

Anthony Lomax (11)
Cheadle RC Junior School

The Playground Is . . .

One minute the playground is . . .
A huge, gaping hole, preparing to swallow me up,
A giant city centre, stuffy and packed,
A never-ending plain, going on for miles
And a dark alleyway where true friends cease to exist.

The next minute the playground is . . .
A glittering, sunny paradise with fluttering fairies everywhere,
The first summer's day of July, laughing in the breeze,
A full bowl of fruit smiling, forcing me to be happy
And a hot air balloon floating against the blue.

Lucy McDermott (11)
Cheadle RC Junior School

Friends

Whenever life gets sad
And you're feeling grey
You can count on a friend
To brighten up your day

If the path is dark
And you've lost your way
You need a guiding hand
To stop you going astray

But if you like to smile
And skip and jump and shout
It is always so much better
If your friends are round about.

Corinne Hutton (8)
Cheadle RC Junior School

The Silly Dinosaur

Dinosaur, dinosaur likes to eat,
Favourite food is children meat.
Licks the bones off the floor,
What a messy dinosaur.

Dinosaur, dinosaur with a big belly,
To make it bigger eats lots of jelly.
'More, more!' he would roar,
What a greedy dinosaur.

Dinosaur, dinosaur, hungry still,
Goes to the cupboard to eat his fill.
Traps his finger in the door,
What a silly dinosaur!

Kate McDermott (8)
Cheadle RC Junior School

A Seasonal Tale

As I slowly unfurl, I stretch my fresh new skin,
I am bursting with new life!
Dancing merrily, I feel glad to be alive!

The sun beats down on me making me feel strong and supreme,
I play in the breeze with my friends.
The golden sun shines through the big blue;
All is well with the world.

As I awaken, I find that my world is cloaked in a rusty, golden glow,
My parents are naked and bare,
My friends and I all drift helplessly, useless, defenceless,
Down, down, down, onto the crisp, conker-studded ground.
Ouch! Don't stand on me, you'll crush my spine!
A fabulous firework flash sends me on my way!

Now I am an elderly gentleman, my skin feels shrivelled and dry,
Like an old elephant's hide.
One last frosty snowdrop sends a shiver down my delicate spine . . .
And I curl up and die at the edge of the forest.
I've had a good life.

What am I?

A leaf.

Olivia Booth (10)
Cheadle RC Junior School

The Sea

The waves like foam crashing onto the rocks
Kites in the air dancing with the waves
Squashed sandcastles in the sea
The sun with a smiley face
Kids digging in the sand
Now I see the sun going down
The shadows start to lengthen against the rock pools
I walk along the beach holding Dad's hand
Maybe it's time to go to rest.

William Shiel (7)
Cheadle RC Junior School

Football

I like football very much,
Sometimes it's a laugh,
It's just the perfect hobby,
It ends up being a blast.

I play for Cheadle and Gatley,
They're quite a good team.
We always play the harder teams,
Our boots don't usually gleam.

This is my first ever team
And hopefully not the last.
If I ever get trials,
I'll be glad if I get past.

The best goal I ever scored
Was right in the corner of the net,
The goalie tried to save it,
But fell in the mud and got wet.

I dream of Man United
As I sleep in my bed,
To play at Old Trafford
In the special colour red.

Matthew Gunn
Cheadle RC Junior School

Monkey Kennings

Tail-swinger,
Tree-clinger,
Banana-snatcher,
Vine-catcher,
Fight-picker,
Salt-licker,
Baby-cuddler,
Rain-huddler.

Daniel Knowles (11)
Cheadle RC Junior School

Homework

Homework,
You can love it,
You can hate it,
You might want to blow it up
Into a hundred tiny pieces.

Homework,
It can be fun,
It can be boring,
It can be easy,
It can be hard.

Homework,
It can by nice 'n' easy,
It can be hard 'n' evil,
It can look up at you
With big, evil, black eyes.
It can look up at you
With big, sweet, brown eyes.

But I just hate homework.
To me, hearing the word homework
Is like hearing my death call!
So whatever you say . . .
I will *always* hate homework.

Sandra Madathilethu (10)
Cheadle RC Junior School

Spring

S ome people have a spring clean
P lants will begin a new life
R oses, daffodils, tulips and trees with blossom, they will bloom again
I t soon will be the start of lent
N othing will stop us having a spring clean
G ardens don't look bare anymore.

Conor Ryan (8)
Cheadle RC Junior School

Football

Football, football, football!
How I love football.
Two boxes, two nets, two penalty spots,
One centre circle, four corner flags
And one centre spot.

Goals, goals, goals!
How I love goals.
I just love the ball shooting
At great speed past the keeper
And into the net.

Leagues, leagues, leagues!
How I love the different leagues.
From the English Premiership
And the Spanish La Liga to
The Italian Serie A and the German Bundesliga.

Football, football, football!
How I love football.
The tension in the gigantic stadium
For ninety minutes.

Matthew Trainor (10)
Cheadle RC Junior School

A Dalmatian Poem

Dalmatian, Dalmatian I love to cuddle
Dalmatian, Dalmatian I promise not to struggle
Dalmatians love to run, they find it very fun
Dalmatians woof, I think they're getting rough
Dalmatian, Dalmatian, beautiful, black and white
Must always treat them right.

Caitriona Dooley (7)
Cheadle RC Junior School

The Four Seasons

Autumn has just gone
And winter is here,
I love this time of the year,
Sometimes we have snow
And sometimes we have rain
And I'm really looking forward
To the spring and summertime again.

Cillian Golden (7)
Cheadle RC Junior School

The Chicken's Wishes

I wish I could be free,
Not laying eggs
And getting my head chopped off.
I wish I could be with my friends,
With a full stomach.
Also, I don't want to be in a hut,
I want to play games,
Not sit in a cage.
I want to be *free!*

Ryan Miskell (11)
Cheadle RC Junior School

The Sea

The sea is like a snake,
Sometimes vicious.

The sea is like a dolphin,
Always on the move.

The sea is like a tiger,
Fast and furious.

The sea is like a kangaroo,
Always leaping about.

Conor Young (11)
Cheadle RC Junior School

The Sea

The sea is a horse.
He gallops up and down the beach all day
Trying to beat invisible opponents.
On a quiet day he grazes on the seaweed.
He kicks the stones along the beach,
Playing ping-pong with the crabs.
When he is angry he moans and groans up the cliff top,
Destroying all in his path.
When you walk across the beach he nibbles at your toes.

Hannah Jefferies (11)
Cheadle RC Junior School

My Hamster's Problem

I may be a hamster, but I do have needs,
I'm imprisoned in a cage and I have to eat weeds.
What I need is a pouch full of nuts,
I'll probably die of hunger knowing my luck.
I just want to be loved, like some already are,
In the morning when you draw the curtains I go, 'Aww.'
I need exercise, but not in that ball,
Because when I get in it, I always crash into a wall.
I need something to play with, like a cuddly toy,
After all I am only a little baby boy.

Charlotte Boardman (11)
Cheadle RC Junior School

Horses

The huntsman rides a great stallion,
The soldiers just ride plain grey,
But the farmer rides an old shabby donkey
To push and pull
But never graze,
Just work hard all day for the farmer's own wage.

Alexandra Heywood (10)
Cheadle RC Junior School

The Sea

The sea is a cheetah,
A very fast runner.
The sea is a flower,
The tide could be high,
But if it changes mood quickly
You may need mouth to mouth.
If it is in a silly mood
You will have fun playing around,
And if it is in a mad mood
You had better get right out.
The cheetah has razor teeth,
Sharper than our own.
If you spot one with your eye
Walk away slowly, you will be alright.

Chris Thorpe (11)
Cheadle RC Junior School

The Donkey's Dreams

I want to be rich and famous
And be a very good friend.
I want to go out there and be popular,
I want a Mercedes Benz.
People think I'm a 'flying, talking donkey',
Like in films and books.
I'm not clumsy like Eeyore
I'm just a normal donkey -
Or at least I think I am.
I don't like people taking me for donkey rides
Though my owners do, because they get money.

Thomas Sokolyk (11)
Cheadle RC Junior School

The Chicken's Complaint

I have no real life.
All I do is sit and lay my eggs.
All I want is a bit of freedom
And to keep my eggs so I can have a family.
Shelter and friends are what I need
And not to bleed when the big axe falls.
Food and hay, so far away,
I must find some soon.
Now as I sit and lay my eggs,
My brother is taken away.
Thud!

That will be me some day!

Callum McAllister (11)
Cheadle RC Junior School

My Best Friend

My best friend has a heart of gold.
I know my secrets are never told.
She always lends a helping hand,
To my problems she listens and understands.

On a rainy day she makes it feel sunny,
She makes me laugh because she is so funny.
Hours of talking on the phone,
I feel that I am never alone.

Me and my friend, we're never apart,
Because she has always been in my heart.
When we're older, we'll still be together,
Because I know we'll be friends forever!

Mary Enright (9)
Cheadle RC Junior School

Swimming

(Inspired by 'Boy Flying' by Leslie Norris)

Swimming,
I saw the blueness of the clear ocean,
I looked up and saw magical chunks of candyfloss,
The graceful beauty of dolphins,
And I am out at sea.

Swimming,
I heard the swishing waves splashing on my ears,
The sound of the wind whistling
And the gulls squawking in the background,
But the one thing that I didn't hear
Was my mum shouting, *'Get ready!'*

Jamie Taylor (10)
Cheadle RC Junior School

My Silly Food

Have you ever seen a tiny bean as big as a tangerine?
Round and orange, squashed in porridge, I would eat it up in one.

Have you ever heard of beans on toast?
It's awfully nice with sugar and spice, I would eat it on my bike.

Have you ever been on a trampoline eating ice cream?
It's awfully nice with rice.

Have you ever seen a massive bean?
I would put it in my tum, but don't show Dad
Cos he'll go mad, you don't want that.

Vicky Newsome (7)
Cheadle RC Junior School

Recycling

R emember recycling is very important,
E veryone should recycle.
C ans can go as well.
Y ou should do your best to keep the environment clean and tidy.
C an you tell me how many of you recycle?
L itter is *bad!*
I n some places it is not very clean.
N ear your home you may have a tip.
G reen places are nice to see.

Emily Wagner (9)
Cheadle RC Junior School

A Winter Poem

Frosty snowflakes in the air,
Children playing everywhere
On a winter's morning.
Nothing to be heard,
Not even a little bird.

In the crystal-white wonderland winter time
Is really grand, the snow is very white,
Snug up for the winter's night.

I look out into the black night sky
To see a white magic land,
Sitting by the fire, hearing carol choir.

I think winter's really great,
Playing snowballs with my mate.

Daniel Harrison (7)
Cheadle RC Junior School

Stockport County FC

Stockport County are the best,
They stand above all the rest.
In Stockport we wear with pride
The blue shirts of our favourite side.

Edgeley Park is the ground we want to be at,
There's never a doubt, it is a true fact.
Stockport County we follow around,
Even when it's not at their home ground.

So many players with fantastic skill,
It's so good to watch, it is just brill.
Win or lose, no matter which,
We are there when they're on the pitch.

Has any sport been so beautiful?
With the colours white and blue,
I wore my scarf around my neck
At Chesterfield and Crewe.

My father was a County fan,
Like my grandfather before,
And at Edgeley Park I love to wear
The scarf my father wore.

County is their name,
When football is the game.
They get the ball and it's in, in, in,
Every game is a win, win, win.

If we won the cup it's all the same,
Cheadle end would sing their fame,
But when the ball's in the back of the net,
County is their name.

Yes, it's true without a doubt,
Stockport County is what we shout about.
We are from Stockport, yes it's true,
But we don't care, because we are the real blue.

Sam Gibbons (9)
Cheadle RC Junior School

A Typical School Day

My alarm clock rings, I don't get out of bed,
So my mum shouts out, *'It's time for school, sleepyhead.'*
I go downstairs and have a piece of toast,
The letterbox flaps, that's the post.
I rush to the door and put my shoes on,
Just a few seconds later, and then I'm gone.

I've just arrived at the school gate,
Only to discover I'm five minutes late!
I'm really scared about getting told off
By the wicked, evil Mrs Goff.
I've finally reached the main school doors,
And it feels as if my life is on pause.

Luckily for me, Mrs Goff wasn't in,
But I still had a lecture from Mr Griffin.
Now it's time for a load of lessons,
Maths, science and a bit of comprehension.
It's only ten minutes until the bell,
And then I get to play with Michael.

It's the end of break and we are going to assembly,
After that, there's nothing but history.
Finally it's time for lunch,
Now we get to munch and crunch.
But the menu's nothing new,
Just potatoes, vegetables and a bit of stew.

Lunch is now finished and we have DT,
Then we have a spot of PE.
All we did in DT was make, make, make,
And in PE we ran until our legs ached.
When my mum came to collect me she said, 'What have you
been doing today?'
I replied, 'Oh, it was just another typical school day.'

Sam Theophanous (9)
Cheadle RC Junior School

Bullies

Bullies think they're grown up,
Bullies think they're cool,
Bullies think they rule the school,
Bullies think we're right fools.

Why me,
Does it have to be,
Me getting bullied?
I'm ever so clever,
So what that I get 100% on a test?
So what the teachers like me?
So what I'm good at maths and technology?

I just want to be a normal person,
How hard can that be?

It's very hard indeed,
To take in their sneers and glares,
The teases
And the name calling,
It's just so appalling.
All this pressure rushes to my head,
Making it feel like a volcano erupting.

But it's not *all* of the bullies' fault,
It's the victims too.
They should stop teasing,
And we should tell someone.

But I know what all of us need,
A caring friend
To help us mend all the rough edges.

But all I wish
Is to be happy and safe in the world.

Clementine Kellaway (10)
Cheadle RC Junior School

The Magic Box

(Based on 'Magic Box' by Kit Wright)

I will put in my box . . .
A speedy, swerving snowboard on ice,
The curve in the Amazon river,
The crack of Indiana Jones' whip.

I will put in my box . . .
100 magical, mesmerizing mermaids singing songs of sadness,
Elaborate feathers of rarest birds,
The happiest times of all.

I will put in my box . . .
The song of the bluest whale,
The silky-soft scales of a frantic flying fish,
The flash of first lightning illuminating the sky.

I will put in my box . . .
A rock, red and roaring from Pluto,
The wave of tides turning in time,
The eruption of Vesuvius the volcano.

My box is fashioned from the blackest ice
With patterns engraved in gold.
Its hinges are two long, lazy lizards.
In the corners are the sun and the moon.

I shall swim in my box in warm, tropical Caribbean seas,
Diving in exquisite coral reefs,
Then rest on the golden beach of an exotic island.

Katharine Roddy (10)
Cheadle RC Junior School

Socks

This poem is true,
I want to share it with you.
I have a cat called Socks,
He doesn't run, he hops.
While going out to play
On a bright sunny day,
A car going past
That was going too fast
Ran over his leg.
I'm so glad he's not dead.
The man said he was sorry
And told me not to worry.
Although he can't run,
He still has some fun,
Hopping around the house
Trying to catch a mouse.
Socks is now nine
And still doing fine.
This poem is for Socks,
The cat who can't run, but hops.

Robert Caldwell (7)
Cheadle RC Junior School

Spring

Spring, spring, beautiful spring,
The pretty flowers dazzle in the sunlight.
Orange, yellow and purple colours everywhere.
Petals fluttering in the wind,
Crisp air at dawn, everything glistens.
Picking daisies and making daisy chains,
Playing, smiling, laughing, having fun.
Newborn lambs bleating.

Samantha Hince (9)
Cheadle RC Junior School

Have You Ever Seen . . . ?

Have you ever seen . . .
A stale sardine
Or a bucket of rotten cod?
I'd eat the lot
Upon the spot,
I'm such a hungry bod.

Have you ever seen . . .
A big baked bean
That's bigger than your mum?
Don't tell your dad
Cos he'll go mad
When he sees your big fat tum.

Have you ever seen . . .
A fairy queen
Sitting on her throne?
She's got a dog,
His name is Bog,
Throw them both a bone.

Have you ever seen . . .
A boy like me
Writing out a rhyme?
I've had some fun,
Sat on my bum,
I hope first prize is mine!

Thomas Fagan (7)
Cheadle RC Junior School

Spring Is Here

S pring is here, hip, hip, hooray,
P retty flowers along the way,
R unning children in the park,
I n the morning I hear the larks.
N o more dark and gloomy nights,
G lad in the morning that it's very light.

Ellie Lavelle (8)
Cheadle RC Junior School

Families

Families can be annoying
And embarrassing too,
Like when you've got your friends round
And they start singing on the loo!

First of all there are mums
Who say, 'Don't break my ornaments!'
When we're in the middle
Of a pillow fight tournament.

After that there's dads
Who ask you to a game of cricket.
He can't really play himself,
As he bowls the ball at the wickets!

Clare White (10)
Cheadle RC Junior School

Barney Sarney

Barney Sarney went to sea
Silver buckles on his knee
He'll come back and marry me
Dodgy Barney Sarney.

He saw seven sporty bears.
Monday's bear runs far and wide,
Sunday's bear, I'm proud to say,
Has just scored a goal.
Hip, hip, hooray!

Sean Connolly (9)
Cheadle RC Junior School

Boy Climbing

(Inspired by 'Boy Flying' by Leslie Norris)

Climbing,
I saw the bottom of the oak tree,
I saw the bright green grass and
The gleaming blue river with all its colourful fish.
I could not see my bedroom,
Or my next-door neighbour playing football outside.
I could not see the busy motorway with all its cars,
Or my house with its red roof.
I felt the gentle breeze on my face,
I felt the scorching sun on my back
And the leaves bristling against my face.

Ben Platt (10)
Cheadle RC Junior School

Boy Fishing

(Inspired by 'Boy Flying' by Leslie Norris)

I saw the dolphin splashing in the blazing sun
And the fish drifting through the water.
I could hear the parrots
Repeating the sound in the background.
I could hear the splash of
The whale's enormous back fin.
I could feel the sea
Drifting past my boat.
I could see the clouds
Drifting over the beautiful sea.

Jordan Goddard (9)
Cheadle RC Junior School

Me Swimming

(Inspired by 'Boy Flying' by Leslie Norris)

Swimming,
I saw the people selling seafood,
I saw the pier with rides on,
I saw the clouds moving
Like boats with white sails
And the sun beaming on me.

Swimming,
I could not see my sausages sizzling in a pan,
I could not see the boys on the front lawn playing football.

Megan Downes (9)
Cheadle RC Junior School

A Dream

I was floating on a cotton cloud,
I could only hear the slightest sound,
The sound of birds flapping,
The sound of waves slapping,
I wish it was true.

I was lying on a bed of thorns,
I could sense my worst smells,
The smell of hands after touching prawns,
The smell of dirty, foul lawns.
I wish I was awake.

Courtney Wright (9)
Cheadle RC Junior School

My Friend Elizabeth

My friend Elizabeth has brown hair and blue eyes,
I always like her, even if she tells lies.
Elizabeth is a nice, kind and sweet child,
I liked her best when she first smiled.
She is really funny,
Sometimes she even acts like a bunny.
She is always my friend, doesn't matter what she does,
And I know she really likes to buzz.
She is my friend and I like her a lot,
So one day I shall give her a magic pot.
She is my best ever friend that I could ever have,
She is my friend and that is that.
She is my friend *Elizabeth!*

Hannah Clayton (8)
Cheadle RC Junior School

Night-Time

Why don't I like the night?
Is quite a funny question,
It's because it's black and white,
Do you have a suggestion?
But the dark can also be these things,
Kind, necessary and beautiful too!
I sometimes have dreams that I have wings,
And remember I stuck my fingers in glue!
But only in the night-time,
So enjoy it while you can,
You might even dream that you were fabulously glam!

Tara Cox (8)
Cheadle RC Junior School

Silence

Silence is snow-white, like a lonely, powdery cloud against the blue.
It sounds like a silent, dilapidated stadium.
It smells like a breath of fresh air . . . at the Lake District.
It feels like you're all alone.
It reminds me of praying at church.
It tastes like bread . . . very plain.
It looks like a road, never-ending . . . suffocated in snow.

Thomas Patching (11)
Cheadle RC Junior School

Little Sisters

Little sisters are lovely to have
Because they are cuddly, cute and sweet.
They chatter and giggle around the place
And waddle around on tiny feet.

She calls my name with a book in her hand,
Then I sit her on my knee.
It's nearly time to go to bed,
After her favourite story.

Kyle Albiston (7)
Cheadle RC Junior School

My Mum

My mum might have a big fat bum,
But I don't care, she is still my mum.

She can be mean, she can be pushy,
And when she kisses me it's very slushy.

My mum might have a big fat bum,
But I don't care, she is still my mum.

Sophie Doyle (8)
Cheadle RC Junior School

My Hamster

My hamster sleeps all day,
All day I play,
My hamster plays all night,
Surely that cannot be right?
My hamster chews nuts and fruit and runs on her wheel,
She runs so fast, sometimes I think she isn't real.
She has a twitchy nose and little feet,
I love my hamster, and keep her cage really neat.

James Robinson (7)
Cheadle RC Junior School

Flowers, Flowers, Flowers

F lowers, flowers, beautiful flowers,
L avender, green, red and white. A pretty sight.
O range flowers you can see. How I love them, so does she.
W onderful flowers make a wonderful smell,
E ach one casting its magical spell.
R ain falling down helps them grow,
S unshine completing the awesome show.

Daniel Beasley (7)
Cheadle RC Junior School

Easter

Easter comes, Easter comes, the bunnies start to hum.
The Easter bunny likes to eat honey.
The trees never breeze,
They all get Easter eggs and they never have to beg.
The Easter bunny stays for tea, to come and see our house.
Then it is Easter time, and then it is Easter time.

Anna Lightfoot (7)
Cheadle RC Junior School

Star

Twinkle, twinkle little star,
How I wonder what you are.
You're just a ball of burning gas,
My dreams are shattered, oh alas!
Shining in the starry night,
I thought you were my guiding light.
To find that you are burning and bubbling,
In my heart that is very troubling.
But when I look at you one more time,
I know I can finish my little rhyme.
How I wonder what you are,
Yes, I know, you're a shining star!

Benjamin McAllister (8)
Cheadle RC Junior School

Snow

Snow, snow, snow,
Wake up, look outside,
Snow is falling on
All of our windows.

See the children
Playing outside,
Look at the snowmen
Emerging from the ground.

See the snowballs
Fly by through the air,
Look at the massive one
Over there.

Look at all of the children
Running for their hot dinners.

Conor Craven (7)
Cheadle RC Junior School

City Boy

He heard cars zoom like a comet,
He heard people chatting about what they saw,
He heard the shop doors open,
He heard the echo of the Metro below him.

He didn't hear the cows mooing,
He didn't hear the plough of the tractor,
He didn't hear the birds singing,
He didn't hear the farmers yawn.

He saw the market in the street,
He saw the beggar with a small cup,
He saw the big wheel going round and round,
He saw the tram rushing by.

He didn't see a horse plodding,
He didn't see the bright green hills,
He didn't see the huge oak tree,
He didn't see the large yellow haystack.

Thomas Donaghy (9)
Cheadle RC Junior School

My Pets

My pets, Buster and Harriet,
So chubby, round and plump.
Buster runs out, pinches a carrot and runs away.

Little oval faces peeping out.
Harriet is the hungry one
And Buster is a scaredy.

Me and my sister love them.
We feed them every day.
Me and my family all *love pets.*

Amy Pullar (7)
Cheadle RC Junior School

Swimming

(Inspired by 'Boy Flying' by Leslie Norris)

Swimming,
She saw the blue bubbles
Floating up from the snorkels
And the lost armband
Of her sister.
She could not see the cars
Zooming down the bumpy roads,
The shoppers dashing for the sales.

Swimming,
She felt the slap of her
Wrinkled hand on her thigh,
And the water of the filter
Pushing her away from the steps.
She could not feel her warm, cosy bed,
Nor her mum's gentle hand.

Megan Grady (10)
Cheadle RC Junior School

My Cat Scoot

I have a cat called Scoot,
And he is rather cute.
He is black and white
And sleeps all day and night.
He is smooth and furry
And when I stroke him, he is rather purry.
He is very soft to touch
And I love him very much.

Isabelle Foley (7)
Cheadle RC Junior School

Boy Swimming

(Inspired by 'Boy Flying' by Leslie Norris)

He saw the cobwebs
Dropping from the rocks
By the water,
But he could not see the spiders.
He could feel the cold breeze
Mopping his skin,
But he could not feel
The joy of being on holiday.
He could hear the playing
Of delighted children,
But he could also hear
Grown-ups and crying babies
Under the sun.

Elliot Clyne (9)
Cheadle RC Junior School

Netball

Netball, netball,
Jump for the ball.
Netball is fun,
It keeps you panting.
You are not allowed to
Move with the ball,
Keep your foot on the spot.
Play the matches
And you will get better,
Then you will score the goals!

Hannah Entwistle (7)
Cheadle RC Junior School

Joe

There once was a boy called Joe,
He had an enormous toe.
It stuck out of his shoe in the snow,
And Joe didn't even know.

Joe always got the school bus,
He was never in a rush
And never caused a fuss,
He liked things to be quiet and hushed.

His friends they used to call,
At his home to play football.
Joe would certainly give his all,
Because he loved this game best of all.

Oliver Clyne (9)
Cheadle RC Junior School

Conor's Dog

Cat-chaser
Fast-pacer

Bone-eater
Fire-heater

Postman-biter
Stray dog-fighter

Fast tail-wagger
Burglar-bagger

Bath-hater
Hair-straighter

Man's friend
The end!

Adam Swales (10)
Cheadle RC Junior School

I Love Rabbits

I love rabbits,
They're lovely and cute.
They have some very funny habits,
I think they're really soft.
I'd like a new bunny
And I'd call him Honey.
They make me smile very much
When they run a mile.
How I love rabbits.
Running around the garden, hoppity-hop,
Watch those big ears go floppity-flop.
I really do love *rabbits!*

Victoria Gorton (7)
Cheadle RC Junior School

Fluffy The Cat

Cats are nice, cats are clean.
Fluffy catches mice, I think she's mean.

She sometimes falls asleep on my lap,
And when she awakes, she takes another nap.

She has one black and three white paws,
And on the end, some very sharp claws.

When she's alone she'll purr and purr,
Then lick and lick and clean her fur.

She's cute and furry and cuddly too,
I love my cat and I'm sure she will love you.

Faith Parker (8)
Cheadle RC Junior School

Weather

W et days aren't nice,
E specially when there's lots of ice.
A ll the children slip and slide
T ogether you can watch them glide.
H orrid days are when it's windy,
E veryone's hair blows like Sindy,
R otten days are when it's windy.

Naomi Tan (8)
Cheadle RC Junior School

Hate

Hate is green like boiling acid.
It smells like burning,
Contaminated, black smoke.
It tastes like ten broccoli
Coated in mayonnaise.
It feels like slipping in front of
100 pupils.
It sounds like a vehicle colliding
With a wall.
It reminds me of the tsunami disaster.
It looks like armed robbers
Breaking into a bank.

Lucas Martin (11)
Cheadle RC Junior School

Snow Falling

Snow is gently floating like a butterfly
Flakes with different patterns
Twirling, whirling in the sky
I looked out the window, everywhere was white
Then I saw some children having a snowball fight.

Alex Charnock (7)
Cheadle RC Junior School

The Game

Pick sides
Wear our strip
Goalie in
Whistle blows
Pass to Damian
Dom to Chris
Chris to Lee
Oh! A tackle
Win it back
Pass to Rob
Rob to Dom
Dom to Reece
Reece to me!
Shoot! Wham!
And it's in!
It's a goal!
Goal!

Gavin Clements
Golborne Primary School

A Natural World

A natural world,
Is full of girls,
There are a couple of boys,
But they look like toys,
There are a few schools,
But no pools,
Schools are full of teachers,
As soft as peaches,
The children are nice,
Like sugar and spice,
The boys are silly,
But none are like Billy,
He's the one with all the ideas,
Jumbled together like mushy peas.

Summer Jones (8)
Golborne Primary School

Wave Of Disaster

Somewhere in the world today a wave kills hundreds . . .
Somewhere in the world today people fall ill and sick
                                        with starvation . . .
Somewhere in the world today people dig for loved ones . . .
Somewhere in the world today helicopters bring in food . . .

Somewhere in the world today, people need *help!*

Zoë Jones (10)
Golborne Primary School

Somewhere . . .

Somewhere in the world today . . .
A pride of lions scavenge over a carcass,
A burrow of bunnies hurry for their food,
A drey of squirrels crack open the shell of an acorn,
A flower with pink petals is growing,

Somewhere . . .

Katie Bilsbury (10)
Golborne Primary School

Our Town

G olborne is the town we live in.
O ld and new houses here and there.
L and and lots of places to go.
B ig houses and lots of shops.
O ur school is Golborne Community Primary.
R ows of streets in a line.
N ight and day comes and goes.
E veryone should live in *Golborne!*

Zoë Draisey (11)
Golborne Primary School

We Were Born . . .

We were born to sing
We were born to be artistic
We were born to be messy
We were born to be kind
We were born to swim
We were born to write
We were born to shop!

Nicole Thompson (7)
Golborne Primary School

The Pet That I Want . . .

The pet that I want . . .
Will have piercing blue eyes,
Will be fluffy and sweet,
Never hurt anyone,
It will have claws like knives,
But will be smart and cute . . .
And jump in the air like a spring,
It will hunt its prey and prowl,
Chase, catch and play . . .
Play with me!

Claire Anders (11)
Golborne Primary School

Hamster

H amster running round the floor
A round the corner and out of the door
M um's vacuuming, 'Get the hamster back
S he's running towards the rubbish sack'
T rap her gently in a cup
E veryone's happy, she's been picked up
R unning round her cage again, Hooray!

Laura Warburton (9)
Kingsley St John's CE Primary School

What Is Christmas All About?

'What is Christmas all about?'
Said the sheep to the cow.
'Is it about Santa on his sleigh?
How do we know, how?'

'What is Christmas all about?'
Said the ox to the ass.
'Is it about the presents
That we get in a mass?'

'What is Christmas all about?'
Said the donkey to the fish.
'Is it about the lights shining bright?
I wish I knew, I wish!'

'What is Christmas all about?'
Said the dove to the lark.
'Is it about the carol singers' lanterns
Twinkling in the dark?'

'I know what Christmas is all about,'
Said the cow to the sheep.
'It's about looking in a manger
And watching Jesus sleep.'

'I know what Christmas is all about,'
Said the ass to the ox.
'It's about peering in a stable
At the Son of God in a box.'

'I know what Christmas is all about,'
Said the fish to the donkey.
'It's about bowing down to
Jesus, every man on his knee.'

'I know what Christmas is about,'
Said the lark to the dove.
'It's about a baby coming down
A baby from above.'

Hannah Goldsby (11)
St Matthew's CE Primary School, Stockport

The Candle Flame

She spreads peace with passion throughout our land,
She guides us in times of gloomy darkness,
She rises high like a sunrise to all cold-blooded evil,
She loves to dance wildly, moving from side to side,
Lighting up our life, she brings hope and joy,
Deep in the valley she tarries,
As long as there is a flame in the candle of justice, she will be
                                                    kind and affectionate,
She brings gentleness and kindness to everyone's heart,
Remembrance, she gives us the strength to remember our
                                                    loved ones,
Her outstanding power holds us together as we stand united,
Her glazing eyes burn brightly and happily as they cheer up a
                                                    disappointed soul,
She will never die as long as we willingly hold . . .
Kindness . . .
Peace . . .
Hope . . .
Love . . .
And joy . . .
In our hearts!

Amber Shun-Shion (11)
Warren Wood Primary School

Bubbles Tanka

Slippery bubbles,
That roll, twist, shake; down, down, down,
Gracefully jumping,
A mirror ball of magic,
Up, down, up down, twist and pop!

Matthew Salt (10)
Warren Wood Primary School

The Candle Flame

Beaming . . .
Glowing . . .
As it stands proudly in the starlit sky,
A flickering flower, fluttering in the sparkling sun,
Dancing and prancing like a great ball of fire in the bottomless
blue ocean,
A colourful, calm butterfly, glimmering in the calm, peaceful air,
Twinkling . . .
Tremendously . . .
As its heavy, burning beam,
Melts in the thick, wide wax,
A colourful contrasting glow waving as the wind breathes heavily,
Peace, calmness, as it spreads wearily,
The flame beams,
Glows . . .
Dies.

Olivia Yates (10)
Warren Wood Primary School

The Candle Flame

She stands secretly glowing,
Gentle and harmless, but constantly flickering,
Longing to move but kept in captivity.
She's tall, amazingly tall,
She's bright, amazingly bright,
But deep down, she's hot and dark,
She's planted tightly in a deep dark ditch,
She sways beautifully and has a loving heart.
She wants to send a message to everyone else,
To carry the hopefulness around the world caringly,
All she wants is more of her all over the world!

Lucy Thomas (11)
Warren Wood Primary School

The Candle Flame

A white chocolate bar dribbling in the sun,
The nib of a yellow pencil glowing in the distance,
Like a skeleton still have their rose in their cheek,
A luminous light glowing on the top of the statue,
The wick like a stem,
The radiant light like a blossom,
The fluorescent smell of the spectacular,
The wick dying,
Burning . . .
Blazing . . .
The wick dies,
Burning . . .
Blazing . . .
The flame is dying,
Burning . . .
Blazing . . .
The *flame* has died.

Michael Lee (11)
Warren Wood Primary School

The Candle Flame

A colourful flower dancing wildly in the cool breeze,
Like a shooting star blazing rapidly through the midnight sky,
The orange basketball ready to be put into the white hoop,
Glowing brightly, through the glass window,
The hot, sweltering fireball melting the Earth,
The calm, gentle flame, going,
going . . .
going . . .
gone!

Dean Normington (11)
Warren Wood Primary School

A Concrete Poem About A Droplet of Water

Drip,
Drop,
Drip, drop,
Spouting out,
Rolling,   slippery,
Trickling down mountains,
Slowly falling into a stream,
..........*S p l a s h*............
Over sharp, jagged rocks,
Getting larger and larger,
Gushing and rushing,
Slowing   down,
Peacefully, calmly,
Drifting   along,
Drip, drop
Drip.

Samantha Bewes (11)
Warren Wood Primary School

A Concrete Poem About A Droplet Of Water

He's plunging;
From the top of the cliff,
He feels he has no power,
But secretly, he's the stronger;
He is innocuous to the demon, fire.
He is travelling at the highest speed,
He stands still, solidly frozen;
As the atmosphere hits a chill
He flies up and up;
As heat passes by
He hits the ground
As he screams,
Ouch!

Joe Robinson (11)
Warren Wood Primary School

The Candle Flame

Dragons' eyes flickering, flapping, telling their life, and bold bravery.
Chimeras' heads, their wide mouths, a flare of light.
The unicorn, galloping, guiding those in doubt to safety,
                            with the floodlight of its horn.
The phoenix, flying above the fluffy forest, the flaming feathers
                                        tell of the danger.
The griffin's treasure, the reflection from the sun spreads hope.
Fairies' wands, the magic tip shines stunningly.
Faithful, fighting, fierce samurais charge to war, but soon the
                            Flames on . . .
                                Their . . .
                                    Swords . . .
                                        Will . . .
                                            Die . . .

Eleanor Cunningham (10)
Warren Wood Primary School

The Candle Flame

A golden lemon dancing, prancing elegantly beneath the great ball
                                        of fire,
Cobras leaping to the music, swaying quietly, softly,
A colourful flick of paint standing upright against the damp wall,
It jumps furiously into the mild air then comes peacefully back
                                        to reality,
The glowing vibrant jelly wobbles like it's never done before,
The autumn-rich coloured leaves falling . . .
Falling . . .
Falling . . .
Resting on the ground,
Floats up to Heaven where its place is found.

Hannah Roberts (11)
Warren Wood Primary School

The Magic Box

(Based on 'Magic Box' by Kit Wright)

I will put in the box
A fast cheetah feeding with its cubs.
In my box is the sun gazing upon the Earth
Legendary eye from the spies from the dead.

I will put in the box
The winning goal in the FA Cup
The starry sky one summer night
And a dragon looking on me trying to eat me.

I will put in the box
Arrows from the dark lord
Who puts evil spells all over the world
It smells like fresh air.

I will put in the box
The rough skin of an elephant
Walking through the grass.

Jack Boswell (7)
Warren Wood Primary School

The Candle Flame

Glittering, dazzling, rising, flashing far in the distant sky,
Glaring eyes staring wide within the darkened mist,
Burning to a point like a wigwam on the plains,
Swishing, swaying from side to side,
Dancing, wobbling under the golden sun,
Flutters . . .
Flickers . . .
Flutters . . .
Ceases to exist.

Georgia Bartosz (10)
Warren Wood Primary School

The Magic Box

(Based on 'Magic Box' by Kit Wright)

I will put in the box . . .
A beautiful glowing phoenix on a glittering hill.
The sun's rays shining on the Earth.
A diamond-backed snake slithering along.
The rough fur of a dazzling cheetah.

I will put in the box . . .
The sound of a golden eagle feeding its young.
The liqueur smells of chocolate.

I will put in the box . . .
The beautiful eyes of a kitten.
The waves crashing against a lighthouse.
The breeze softly touching my face.

I will put in the box . . .
An angry monster running after me.
A fox stealing chickens.
A dog playing in the sun.

Jake Norris (7)
Warren Wood Primary School

The Candle Flame

A bright, long light, blooming like a flower,
A sharp, shiny knife reflecting off the sun,
A long, straight wick burns from top to bottom,
A dragon's tail waving in the wind; dancing like a fish,
Still, silent sun; reflecting over a large furry forest,
The watery, silky wax dribbles slow and silent down a firm side,
The flame flickers. . .
Flickers . . .
Flickers . . .
Dies.

Jack Rae (10)
Warren Wood Primary School

The Magic Box

(Based on 'Magic Box' by Kit Wright)

I will put in the box . . .
Shiny silver on a starry night.
The rough skin of a snake.
The taste of cherries ripening on a bush.

I will put in the box . . .
The cold of an ice cream on a hot summer day.
Shimmering gold in the moonlight.
The crashing waves on high rocks.

I will put in the box . . .
The sight of an ancient bird staring at me.
The fire from the hottest volcano.
The singing from a bird in the spring.

I will put in the box . . .
The smell of a water spring.
The Earth spinning in my hand.
Fruit bigger than houses.

My box is . . .
Decorated with ancient patterns.
Alien signature in other languages.
Secrets in all dark corners.

Ben Gardiner (7)
Warren Wood Primary School

The Candle Flame

A bubbly, light ball glittering in the midnight sky,
The shining sun right in your eyes,
The waves gently coming, coming straight at you,
A colourful angelfish swimming elegantly through the sea,
A little dancing and prancing star,
A little bunny rabbit hopping through the lovely green grass,
A straight, straight statue standing in the middle of the country,
A flame's burning . . . burning . . . burning and then it dies.

Lucy Stead (10)
Warren Wood Primary School

The Magic Box

(Based on 'Magic Box' by Kit Wright)

I will put in the box . . .
The green grass from the back of a big factory.
The rough skin from a charging rhino.
The smooth skin of a brown puppy dog.

I will put in the box . . .
The sound of a husky dog in winter.
The red eyes on a vampire's face.

I will put in the box . . .
Petrol that smells of strong mints.
The stormy weather on the beach.

I will put in the box . . .
A racing car going past on the race tracks.

I will put in the box . . .
Gold, silver and bronze medals.
The whole universe.
A big bowling alley.

My box is full of shiny gold secrets hidden in the corners.
Freaky when you hold it in your hand.

Liam Thomas Cocks (7)
Warren Wood Primary School

The Candle Flame

Two golden stems with red and orange leaves,
A person standing elegantly with orange hair,
Two ferocious dragon's eyes glaring terrifyingly,
Some stars shining soundless in the blowing air,
A light bulb standing tall with a sharp pencil point,
The flame flickers . . .
Flickers . . .
Flickers . . .
Dies!

Samantha Willows (11)
Warren Wood Primary School

Earth Kennings

Country spinner
Day catcher
Night catcher
Grass swisher
Wave roarer
Fish shimmer
Sunlight bomber
Lightning frightener
Wind blower
Frost cracker
Rain wetter
Snow faller
Animal grower
River flower
Reservoir cleaner
Earth spinner.

Molly Foster (10)
Warren Wood Primary School

The Candle Flame

A mini light that leaks, slowly twisting and turning through the air,
The gentle breeze lighting the midnight sky,
A lioness, razor-sharp claws waving so, so suddenly through

the grass.

A silent child whispering to her noble friend,
The bright orange that has just been peeled,
The flame twists

turns . . .
twists . . .
turns . . .
burns . . .
dies!

Fallon Mathieson (11)
Warren Wood Primary School

Earth Kennings

Sphere rotator,
Rain absorber,
Life giver,
Soil killer,
Plant rotter,
Floating spinner,
Keeper of peace,
Element keeper,
Wood compactor,
Coal maker,
Fire spreader,
Water splasher,
Wind blower,
Animal lover,
Moon friend,
The Earth.

Bradley Cook (11)
Warren Wood Primary School

The Candle Flame

The beaming orange sunlight glowing in the distance,
The blistering fire struggles for breath,
The wax weeps and dribbles down the candle,
The continuous flame flickers on and off,
The flame droops with weakness and
Flickers . . .
Flickers . . .
Flickers . . .
Dies!

Tom Carey (10)
Warren Wood Primary School

The Magic Box

(Based on 'Magic Box' by Kit Wright)

I will put in the box . . .
The sight of a big giraffe striding majestically through the trees.
The smell of bread just come out of the oven.
The sound of rain tapping on the window.

I will put in the box . . .
The sight of the sun going down on a hill,
Red, orange and yellow.
The dream of an angel talking to me.

I will put in the box . . .
Melted chocolate on a dish.
A shining moon on a dark night.
The feel of a rough, bumpy piece of grass.

My box is . . .
Always colourful
My box is very brilliant because it shows me my last moments.

I shall play with my friends in my box and
I shall hug my mum and my family.
I shall also climb trees in my box.

Hannah Maxwell (7)
Warren Wood Primary School

The Candle Flame

A golden plant with bursting buds glowing in the sun,
The yolk of an egg gleaming under the gas fire,
A big, juicy orange sitting on top of a yellow banana,
The shooting, golden star firing through space,
A yellow hot air balloon drifting up into the light blue sky,
The flame flies and flickers . . .
                    Flickers . . .
                    Flickers . . .
                    Away.

Scott Williams (11)
Warren Wood Primary School

The Magic Box

(Based on 'Magic Box' by Kit Wright)

I will put in the box . . .
A roaring of a lion.
The sun in New York.
A vulture ripping up its prey.
The brightness of the stars.

I will put in the box . . .
The wetness of water.
The burning of the sunlight.
A foot kicking a ball.

I will put in the box . . .
A caveman shouting.
Someone swimming in the sea.
People laughing at a party.

My box is covered with red paint.
My box has ancient snakes guarding it.

Owen Burslam (7)
Warren Wood Primary School

The Candle Flame

The flame is a . . .
A great ball of fire shooting and gliding about,
A samurai warrior's sword gleaming in the moonlight,
Golden daffodils' petals whose scent is glorious,
A beam of light from a torch,
A child dancing in the dark,
Stars twinkling in the distance.

Tears of forgiveness dribbling down its cheek
Sadly, it flickers . . .
Flickers . . .
And dies.

Daniel Goodwin (10)
Warren Wood Primary School

The Magic Box

(Based on 'Magic Box' by Kit Wright)

I will put in the box . . .
The power of the sun that shines on the Earth.
The excitement of a cheetah speeding through the grass.
The eagle screeching through the wood.

I will put in the box . . .
The smell of the salted ocean.
Dreams that mean something to me
And the colour purple that reminds me of a baby.

I will put in the box . . .
The feelings of making good friends.
Summers that make children play on the beach.
Coming face to face with a black dragon.

I will put in the box . . .
The fresh food that makes us live.
The wind from tornadoes.
Men bungee-jumping off a skyscraper.

My box is ancient from the North Pole.
My box is sewn by an Indian.
The leather is made by an African girl.

Dean Leadbeater (8)
Warren Wood Primary School

Bubbles Tanka

Transparent bubble,
Floats slowly through atmosphere,
Prancing in the air,
Trails soggy, soapy, glitters,
Spinning, swerving down *pop, pop!*

Liam O'Brien (10)
Warren Wood Primary School

The Magic Box

(Based on 'Magic Box' by Kit Wright)

I will put in the box . . .
A sound of a bee flying around me.
A dog licking his brown fur.
I hear music in my ears in the corners of my box.

I will put in the box . . .
The bright sunshine in my shiny eyes.
An angry dragon breathing his smelly breath on me.
A room of monsters looking at me.

I will put in the box . . .
A full box of warming cups of tea.
I dream of putting a black pony in my box.

I will put in the box . . .
A sun and dark rain.
A shiny apple.
I can see a box sparkling at me.

My box is . . .
Pink and red and gold and it sparkles in the sun and makes me
feel happy.

Sophie Torkington (8)
Warren Wood Primary School

Bubbles Tanka

Transparent bubbles
Multicoloured, soggy spheres
Huge outlined circles
Light shining, rainbow balls; they
Will always bring happiness.

Jackie Liu (10)
Warren Wood Primary School

The Magic Box

(Based on 'Magic Box' by Kit Wright)

I will put in the box . . .
the light of a damp, colourful rainbow,
the friendly face of my teacher, Miss Jones
and the cuddliness of my cute, soft hamster.

I will put in the box . . .
the strong colour of dark blue
the lightness of bright yellow
and the multicoloured light from the Earth.

I will put in the box . . .
a dream that could never be dreamed,
a dream with lots of light in it
and a dream that isn't really there.

I will put in the box . . .
the sweet chirp of a happy bird,
the loud bark of a delightful dog
and the lovely miaow of a newborn baby kitten.

My box is fashioned from violets and corn.
It has moon dust in its corners.

Emily Roberts (7)
Warren Wood Primary School

Bubbles Tanka

Prancing, glittering,
Tiny lights reflecting off,
Circular and round,
Popable and too fragile,
Round and round spiralling. *Pop!*

Ian Baguley (10)
Warren Wood Primary School

The Magic Box

(Based on 'Magic Box' by Kit Wright)

I will put in the box . . .
The feel of a cheetah's golden tooth.
The feel of the lovely bright shining moon.

I will put in the box . . .
The blue and silvery dust.
An old gold beautiful, shining coin.
The drifting, sparkling waterfall falling from the rocks.
The watery rain falling from the sky.

I will put in the box . . .
Shining orange sunset.
The sight of the bright moon and twinkling stars.

My box is . . .
Small and not very big,
It is blue and silver and it is the best box in the world.
I shall hide it in my bedroom and never ever let anybody
　　　　　　　　　　　　　　　　　look inside it.

If they do, they will not see anything inside
And I will get them if they dare look inside.

Lewis Mitchell (7)
Warren Wood Primary School

The Magic Box

(Based on 'Magic Box' by Kit Wright)

I will put in the box . . .
the noise of a bird singing in an apple tree
a herd of animals as they all run by
the excitement of going to Chester Zoo.

I will put in the box . . .
the boiling hot air to make you sweat
the cold taste of a cup of milk
a juicy watermelon bigger than the moon.

I will put in the box . . .
the rough skin of a rhinoceros as it gallops by,
the smooth fur of a rabbit as it hops away
the shiniest silver in the world!

I will put in the box . . .
the smell of five rainbow fish swimming in the sea,
the brightest gold in the whole world
a dazzling angel singing to me in the sky.

My box is smooth and soft as the silk slides down,
the summer secrets are all around me,
the pointy arrows stick out like needles.

Keira Amber Mistry (7)
Warren Wood Primary School

The Magic Box

(Based on 'Magic Box' by Kit Wright)

I will put in the box . . .
A mother's first gentle lullaby to a sweet baby
                                    above the rainbow high.
God's unknown face.
A gleaming egg of a golden bird.

I will put in the box . . .
The day my dog Bo ran to school.
The memories that are forgotten.

I will put in the box . . .
A beach of golden sand.
A magnificent sun.
My black dog Bo who dances when I clap.

I will put in the box . . .
A soaring eagle.
The day I got gold in gymnastics.
A field full of animals.

I shall ride on a pony.
Soar through the fields full of animals.
Play with my dog.
Bring my family with me.

Hannah McMurray (7)
Warren Wood Primary School

The Magic Box

(Based on 'Magic Box' by Kit Wright)

I will put in the box . . .
My cheerful little brother I see after a hard day.
The magnificent white moon in the sky so bright.
My super friends that I play with at school.

I will put in the box . . .
The tasty strawberry that is so red and juicy.
The dream I dreamt that I was playing a part in a pantomime.
The colour purple that looks so warm.

I will put in the box . . .
The smell of butter melting on toast.
The coldness of ice cream that makes me cold.
The colour blue that reminds me of ice.

I will put in the box . . .
My brother who plays and looks so cute.
My cuddly teddy bear that's fluffy and brown.
The orangey orange that is so cuddly and warm.

My box is covered with pink, shiny silk.
It has hinges made of sparkling pearls that sparkle
                              like dewdrops in the morning.
When I open the box I get a tingling magic feeling.

I shall dance in my box with all my friends.
I shall have a party and stay up late.
We will keep dancing until my mum says, 'Stop!'

Rachael Warrender (8)
Warren Wood Primary School

The Magic Box

(Based on 'Magic Box' by Kit Wright)

I will put in the box . . .
the friendly voices of my loving parents,
the warm colour of deep blue,
the relaxing colour of lavender.

I will put in the box . . .
the warm summer beach as the sun goes down,
the hot beach sand between my toes,
the soft swishing of a calm sea.

I will put in the box . . .
my relaxing wooden boat in a wilderness of sea,
my tidy white veterinary surgery,
the soft fur of my Syrian hamster.

I will put in the box . . .
the salty smell of the sea,
the delicious smell of freshly baked bread,
the sleepy smell of lavender.

My box is made from crystal-clear water from the deepest ocean,
red beads from the centre of the Earth.

I shall farm in my box,
wake each morning to the call of an elegant cockerel,
then ride a black mare all round my flocks and herds.

Ellen Taylor   (8)
Warren Wood Primary School

The Magic Box

(Based on 'Magic Box' by Kit Wright)

I will put in the box . . .
the sound of the singing sea running across a yellow beach,
the amazing colours of a magical rainbow in the sky,
the lovely smell of flowers in the spring.

I will put in the box . . .
the weather of the cold winter snow dropping on the ground,
the smell of salty seawater crashing on the rocks,
the spectacular texture of smooth shells rustling.

I will put in the box . . .
the sight of my sister's cute little smile,
the golden sunset in the night sky,
the food from a lovely meal when I go out.

My box is orange with stars from the mountaintops,
it's got diamonds in its corners and one in the middle,
my box came from a witch on a stormy night.

I shall swim in my box under the deepest waters,
and over the highest waves,
then wash onto a pale yellow beach,
the colour of shells and the blazing sun.

Hannah Wilson (8)
Warren Wood Primary School

The Magic Box

(Based on 'Magic Box' by Kit Wright)

I will put in the box . . .
A pretty, beautiful pattern from the deepest, darkest crack on Earth.
The colour of bright shining red.
A diver diving into a waterfall.

I will put in the box . . .
A cat with a sparkly tail.
A golden book and a beautiful chair.
A sparkling gleaming blue pool.

I will put into the box . . .
A pool with dirty black suntan in it.
A sea with old salt in it.
A coat with a beautiful snowman in it.

My box is a nice shiny colour yellow.
The red looks like red and gold.
My box looks a nice flowery one.

I shall keep the box forever and ever.
I shall keep it nice and safe.
I shall put the box on my bookshelf in my room.

Jack Thornbury (7)
Warren Wood Primary School

The Magic Box

(Based on 'Magic Box' by Kit Wright)

I will put in the box . . .
the way the salty sea crashes on the beach,
the cool colour of a light blue sky,
and the sounds of birds chirping to each other.

I will put in the box . . .
the smell of nail varnish remover going up my nose,
the happy feeling I get if City wins a football match,
and the colour of dark, deep red.

I will put in the box . . .
the misty world after Bonfire Night,
a sunny day on the beach,
and a tiny smiling newborn baby.

My box is made of gold, silver and bronze,
there is ice in the cracks and water on the lid,
and secrets in the water.

I shall have a zoo in my box and look after and make friends
                                          with the animals.
I shall explore the jungle of frogs, snakes and fish,
I shall keep the animals as pets and I will let them go wild.

Alice Hillen (8)
Warren Wood Primary School

The Magic Box

(Based on 'Magic Box' by Kit Wright)

I will put in the box . . .
the cakes rising in the oven,
the first laugh of a smiley baby
the soft feeling of a nice sponge cake.

I will put in the box . . .
the lovely rich, blue sea
the nice breeze of a windy day
the happy feeling of eating a big cake.

I will put in the box . . .
the birds singing sweetly in the breeze
the first taste of a chocolate
the swishing trees.

I will put in the box . . .
the amazing sight of the beautiful Statue of Liberty
the eerie howling of wolves.

My box is made from blue paint
it's also covered in green feathers
there is also yellow silk on my box.

I shall put in my box a bright light
and a friendly ghost with a howling face.

Rachel Orr (7)
Warren Wood Primary School

The Magic Box

(Based on 'Magic Box' by Kit Wright)

I will put in the box . . .
the sight of all my friends smiling happily,
the thought of little baby Tyler having fun,
the sound of a silent miaow.

I will put in the box . . .
the sound of my friends giggling happily,
the dream of me being an explorer and exploring the jungle,
the colour of the darkest blue that is around.

I will put in the box . . .
the smell of my dad's lovely tea,
the very light blue, as light as light can be,
the touch of my cat, Kieler, rubbing his soft tail across my face.

My box is made out of golden star liquid,
it has sparkling, dazzling butterflies on it,
it has sparkling, white doves on it.

I shall explore in my box,
I shall explore down into deep dark Africa,
I shall explore in the whitest of Antarctica.

Kirsten Muat (7)
Warren Wood Primary School

The Magic Box

(Based on 'Magic Box' by Kit Wright)

I will put in the box . . .
the sight of my cheerful little brother smiling,
the sound of the crashing sea through a smooth shell,
the chew of chewing gum.

I will put in the box . . .
the first word of a bouncing baby,
the sad feeling of having to go to school and leave my family,
the cloudy days and nights in December.

I will put in the box . . .
the chance to fly over the whole world,
to swim the deepest ocean,
to climb the highest tree,
to explore the biggest jungle in the world.

My box is fashioned from wood, metal and plastic,
with flowers in the corner of the lid
and a butterfly in the middle.

I shall play in my box in the warm sunshine,
fly into space, do my work really fast,
swim in a pool in Egypt,
ride a wild tiger from Africa.

Lucy Hanson (7)
Warren Wood Primary School

The Magic Box

(Based on 'Magic Box' by Kit Wright)

I will put in the box . . .
The rough waves gushing onto the bright yellow beach.
The fresh, salty seaweed drying in the bright sun.
I can see dolphins splashing in the sea.

I will put in the box . . .
The relaxation for me on the yellowy beach.
The smell of fish and chips on the beach.
The crashing waves shining in the moonlight.

I will put in the box . . .
The glittery fish playing near the seabed.
(I want to be on the beach right now).
The sun in the sky with a shiny smile.

I will put in the box . . .
The waves going to the end of the ocean.
The feeling of relaxation.

My box is a shiny yellow, gold and blue.
The lid is shiny with swirls.
I shall keep it because it is secret and is special to me.
I can swim in my magic box.

Charlotte Haye (7)
Warren Wood Primary School

The Magic Box

(Based on 'Magic Box' by Kit Wright)

I will put in the box . . .
My gorgeous cat rubbing his head against me.
The view of the faraway horizon at sea
The sight of the spreading daylight zooming.

I will put in the box . . .
The smell of the high-grown tall flowers.
The scent of roses and the sun helping the Earth wake up.
The drifting smell of my glorious breakfast.

I will put in the box . . .
The sound of my brand new alarm clock when it rings.
The echoing sound of cuckoos singing.
Two stars from the highest place in the sky.

My box is fashioned from platinum, gold and steel,
With magic mirrors on the sides and the top,
And expensive rubies on the sides to make it shiny.

I shall ride in my box, seeing my past.
And all the time since I was born
And all my happy excitements.

Harry Crawford (8)
Warren Wood Primary School

The Magic Box

(Based on 'Magic Box' by Kit Wright)

I will put in the box . . .
the view of the amazing Eiffel Tower,
the sounds of birds in the morning,
the smell of a nice new summer's morning.

I will put in the box . . .
the feeling of a nice warm cat,
the happy feeling when I see my baby cousin for the first time,
the nice, bright yellow of the sun.

I will put in the box . . .
a drop of water from Niagara Falls,
a branch of the upside down tree.

I will put in the box . . .
a piece of the moon when it's full,
a piece of sinking sand from the desert,
a little bit of scale from the scary Loch Ness monster.

My box is made from an ancient tyrannosaurus,
on the lid, a scale from a fire dragon,
on the side of the box, a piece from the sun.

Sam Harland (7)
Warren Wood Primary School

The Magic Box

(Based on 'Magic Box' by Kit Wright)

I will put in the box . . .
Red sparkles from spectacular Mars and Jupiter.
Chinese feathers wrapped round a dazzling red ribbon.
White shining corals from the wild Atlantic.

I will put in the box . . .
The sound of the lovely lake drifting by.
A challenging battle (Romans and Celts).
I will retire to a peaceful life in a secret world.

I will put in the box . . .
The sight of seeing my cute baby cousin.
The country smell of the wildlife park.
The sound of trees rustling in the park.

My box is a special one,
It is coloured with red, blue, green, yellow and purple.
It's full of amazing things. The hinges are like rats' claws.

I shall look after my box and take care of it.
I shall drive in it.

Tom Dowse (7)
Warren Wood Primary School

The Magic Box

(Based on 'Magic Box' by Kit Wright)

I will put in the box . . .
the sight of the beautiful Statue of Liberty,
the look of the film the 'Wild Atlantic',
the hope of some violet petal wishes from Heaven above.

I will put in the box . . .
silver beads from the craters of the glorious moon,
dancing doves from up in golden trees.

I will put in the box . . .
a bronze colour from the dusty desert,
a yellowy colour from the fiery sunset,
a pink flower from the Ibiza sea.

I will put in the box . . .
Some very fine linen,
an Indian clock from India,
a smell of some very yummy pizza.

My box is a magic box and it's the god of magic and love,
my box has golden stars on the front,
it has Heaven inside it.

Charlotte Hackney (7)
Warren Wood Primary School

The Magic Box

(Based on 'Magic Box' by Kit Wright)

I will put in the box . . .
the sound when the tall Big Ben strikes twelve,
and the smell of purple forget-me-nots when I put them to my nose,
also the soft fur off the back of my hamster's warm back,

I will put in the box . . .
a dream of having a soft, small Scottie dog licking my face,
the proud feeling when I see my work's alright,
and the blowing breeze in my face on a cold and windy morning.

I will put in the box . . .
the snow mountains of Scotland that are tall and cold,
and the taste of a Chinese meal when it's hot and warm,
also the cold, light blue that is the colour of the deep sea.

My box is . . .
silver and gold and the lid has pearls of any oyster down in the sea,
the hinges are made out of the melted light of the moon.

I shall ride in my box on my black, strong, stallion horse,
and end up in a light forest deep in the woods, the colour of grass.

Megan Sargent (8)
Warren Wood Primary School

The Magic Box

(Based on 'Magic Box' by Kit Wright)

I will put in the box
the biggest dinosaur that has ever lived on Earth,
the sight of a ferocious battle raging everywhere,
the fear of a deserted tower full of ghosts and shadows.

I will put in the box
the smell of delicious French fries waiting for me to eat,
the scent of a raging fire getting closer all the time,
the sniffles of a man crying over his child's grave.

I will put into the box
the feeling of bronze armour and a sword in my hands,
the stroking of a massive battle horse,
the warmth of a fire on my hand in the evening.

My box is made by wood elves and chubby dwarfs
with diamonds on the front and spots on the sides.
It has patterns from the deepest crack in the Earth.

I shall explore the entire world in my box,
having many great adventures in it.
I shall see every single animal on Earth
and then land on my house's doorstep in it.

Matthew Heywood (8)
Warren Wood Primary School

The Magic Box

(Based on 'Magic Box' by Kit Wright)

I will put in the box
the sight of a ferocious battle in my lounge,
the delicious smell of liver cooking in a blazing oven,
a Chinese dumpling that is blazing hot.

I will put in the box
My terrifying dreams of Count Olaf,
a Chinese pork breast in a sticky sauce,
the lovely texture of Chinese noodles.

I will put into the box
the sound of swords clashing,
the smell of horseradish,
the scent of rotten apples.

My box is orange with bright, shiny hinges
that attach the lid to the magic box
it has bumps on the bottom and fabric on the top.

I shall battle in my box around the corner
from a Roman battle site
and end up with the enemy pulling back
back to their homes
back to the city, never to be seen again.

Robert Finch (7)
Warren Wood Primary School

The Magic Box

(Based on 'Magic Box' by Kit Wright)

I will put in the box
A ruby stone worth millions of pounds
A lake in the sunset at a lovely time
the sea at night when the waves rustle.

I will put in the box
A purple star that lights up the dark at night
An eagle that goes faster than thunder
America where sunshine goes.

I will put in the box
My own planet in space
so I could see all the stars so bright
So I had powers and then I could help people
A new magic box with even more powers.

I will put in the box
A kingdom of my own with my own knights
My own story written like Roald Dahl
My own Statue of Liberty.

My box is
Made of blue crystals from the flaming stars

I shall go in my box
To the sea on a very sunny day
Where the water laps on my toes.

Jamie Mitchell (8)
Warren Wood Primary School

The Magic Box

(Based on 'Magic Box' by Kit Wright)

I will put in the box
The bright light of a seaside town,
The scary movie of petrifying 'Shaun of the Dead'.

I will put in the box
The nervous excitement when I score a goal
The anxiety of a person jumping off a cliff
The unselfish gift of my sister.

I will put into the box
A lick of liquorice from the candy shop
The extraordinary T-rex in the museum
The five stars in the sky.

My box is an aeroplane flying up in the sky
With brown wings -
A rumbly, scaring tube full of wonder.

I shall play football day by day
I will climb the highest hill
I shall dive when I am older in the deepest pool
And I shall help people when they are ill.

James Lyons (8)
Warren Wood Primary School

The Magic Box

(Based on 'Magic Box' by Kit Wright)

I will put in the box . . .
A little kitten playing with a ball of string.
I can feel a little kitten when I pick up my box.

I will put in the box . . .
The light of the morning sun when it's shining on the Earth.

I will put in the box . . .
A wish that I could swim with a blue whale.

I will put in the box . . .
The excitement when Molly comes round to my house.

My box is made from silk and ice so I can see all my family.

I shall sing in my box and dance when winning awards as well
and go to the moon and see the stars.

Laura Carey (8)
Warren Wood Primary School

The Magic Box

(Based on 'Magic Box' by Kit Wright)

I will put in the box . . .
the fancy feeling of magic.

I will put in the box . . .
a pretty pattern from the deepest crack in the Earth.

I will put in the box . . .
a glimmer of gold jewellery.

I will put in the box . . .
silver beads from the craters of the moon.

My box is crystal-clear but nobody can see inside
it is blue inside
it is as blue as the summer sky.

I shall dance in my box
with a butterfly fluttering around.

Molly Benson (7)
Warren Wood Primary School

The Magic Box

(Based on 'Magic Box' by Kit Wright)

I will put in the box . . .
The soft ribbon swaying across my hand.

I will put in the box . . .
The feel of my dog's rough fur.

I will put in the box . . .
The sound of a dragon guarding the diamonds.
A big roar from its fiery breath.

I will put in the box . . .
The smell of a Christmas dinner lying on the table.

My box is . . .
Made from ice so I can see through it.
I shall be able to see all my diamonds.

I shall keep it in my secret drawer.

Kimberley Lendon
Warren Wood Primary School

The Magic Box

(Based on 'Magic Box' by Kit Wright)

Rough, touch the beads rolling side to side.
I see the water coming up from my toes every day.
I smell the water and sand on the beach.

I will put in the box . . .
people talking,
sweet wrappers rustling in the breeze,
and the smell of fish and chips.

I will put in the box . . .
adventures on the beach,
waves splashing on the silver-hot rocks.

I will put in the box . . .
sunny, light, lovely places.

My box is private because no one can open it.

Katie Davies (8)
Warren Wood Primary School

The Magic Box

(Based on 'Magic Box' by Kit Wright)

I will put in the box . . .
the sounds of my adorable kitten miaowing in the distance for me
the smell of new fresh bread in the boiling oven.

I will put in the box . . .
the happy feeling when I see my super mum and dad
the feeling of a smooth baby's skin.

I shall put in the box . . .
the sight of a marvellous teacher as she smiles at me
the hot summer weather starting in June.

I will put in the box. . .
the glowing river of the Mississippi as it passes me
the smell of bursting flowers coming out in spring.

My box is made out of gold, silver and the sparkle of bronze,
it has beads on the top and inside there is magic all around.

I shall dance in my box as everybody claps and cheers
in the wide open hall.

Jessica Lee (8)
Warren Wood Primary School

The Magic Box

(Based on 'Magic Box' by Kit Wright)

I will put in the box . . .
a swish of a Chinese dragon,
Mrs Eastham, my best teacher.

I will put in the box . . .
silver beads from the craters of the moon,
sparkling diamonds from the bottom of the sea.

I will put in the box . . .
pure purple silk from the mountains of Nepal,
the speed of a cat.

I will put in the box . . .
the smell of bacon first thing in the morning,
the Northern Lights.

My box is coloured with blue and pink crystals.

I shall fly in my box
up high into the clouds to visit my grandad in the sky.

Rebecca Howarth (8)
Warren Wood Primary School

The Magic Box

(Based on 'Magic Box' by Kit Wright)

I will put in the box . . .
the lovely sunset on the smashing beach,
the amazing sight of dolphins in the deepest sea,
the calm feeling when I stroke my teddy's rough fur.

I will put in the box . . .
the dry, soft sand running on my ticklish fingers,
the smell of salty water on the sandy beach.

I will put in the box . . .
the fabulous colours of the eastern rainbow,
the ruby-red colours of the sunset,
the very first word of a bouncing baby.

My box is pure white silk from the mountains of Nepal,
the last ruby is on my box,
my box has golden walls and a frosty floor.

Jodie Carla Wild (8)
Warren Wood Primary School

The Magic Box
(Based on 'Magic Box' by Kit Wright)

In the box I will put . . .
a Chinese dragon opening its mouth and breathing fire,
the flames firing all over the place and flying to the castle.

I will put in the box . . .
the sound of a lion roaring from the top of a hill
and the blue sea pushing against the rocks.

I will put in the box . . .
a smell of the air pushing against my face and running in the light,
I see a horse galloping in the north wind.

My box is made of bright gold and silver glass
and filling the box up with magical wonders.

I shall swim in my box
and meet an octopus swimming in the sea
and swim with the dolphins and catch with a ball.

Lucas Hilton (7)
Warren Wood Primary School

The Magic Box

(Based on 'Magic Box' by Kit Wright)

I will put in the box . . .
a gloomy eye from a ghost,
the smell of a bonfire,
an old man screaming for help.

I will put in the box . . .
the brightness of the hot sun,
a big guard man,
if you touch it, it feels strange.

I will put in the box . . .
the sound of the sea far, far away,
the spikes of a Chinese dragon,
shiny gold from a shark's tooth.

My box is all the colours in the world.
It's the scariest box in the world as well
and it has everything in the world in it.

Joe Grainger (8)
Warren Wood Primary School

The Magic Box

(Based on 'Magic Box' by Kit Wright)

I will put in the box . . .
the brightness of the big, red sun.
It looks like a real leopard is inside!
The feeling of smooth leopard skin.

I will put in the box . . .
the sound of an angry leopard growling.
A giraffe strolling through the jungle.
A salty ocean crashing together!

I will put in the box . . .
the stinky smell of a McDonald's cheeseburger.
Every day that is sunny and lovely.
The flashing signs of Las Vegas.

I will put in the box . . .
the dream of the last ancient cat.
The bright colours of a long, glowing rainbow.

Daniel Mackenzie (8)
Warren Wood Primary School

The Magic Box

(Based on 'Magic Box' by Kit Wright)

I will put in the box . . .
a gorgeous bonfire with beautiful sparks
a dragon blowing yellow fire
a golden flower from a sparkling waterfall.

I will put in the box . . .
an old coin in my hand
a snake hissing straight at me
a noble unicorn looking around.

I will put in the box . . .
old songs floating around the box
a ripe apple from a magic tree
a starry sky with a silver moon.

I will put in the box . . .
an ancient bird looking angrily at me
a furious giant from a black sky
a magic fairy from fairy world.

My box is made out of brilliant plastic and decorated
with silver stars and it is painted ocean-blue as well.

Shannon Brealey (8)
Warren Wood Primary School

The Magic Box

(Based on 'Magic Box' by Kit Wright)

I will put in the box . . .
the delicious smell of a chocolate factory,
the feeling of the spiky grip tape on a skateboard
and the sight you see.

I will put in the box . . .
the wonderful colour of red and blue,
and the taste of sweeties and chocolate
and the cold, snowy days.

I will put in the box . . .
the sound of my brother giggling,
the nightmare where zombies attack me,
when I dream about being a pro skateboarder.

I will put in the box . . .
when my brother and I have a snowball fight.

My box has a fiery dragon face on the top of it.
I shall skateboard on ramps in the box.

Oliver Woodall (8)
Warren Wood Primary School

My Friend Julie

Julie liked boys,
She had about 100 after her at the most
And she always felt she needed to boast.
They always told her that she was oh so pretty,
So she felt that this should be recorded in this little ditty.

Rebeca Cashin (9)
Woodley Junior School

Is Anybody There

When the moon has come up
And the sun has gone to bed
Everybody but one
Has gone to rest their head.

He packs his past and off he goes
Where he's heading, nobody knows
Fear and sadness, heard in his moans
Filling the emptiness with his heartbroken groans

He leaves behind a darkening city
Striding out with thoughts of pity
Gazing back into the distance
Remembering his every instance
Seeing everyone he ever saw

He is a traveller now
Nobody, no more.

When the moon has come up
And the sun has gone to bed
Everybody but one
Has gone to rest their head.

He's tied his life in a great big knot
That's become undone
But cares, he does not

Eyes wide open
No future he sees
Walking with faith
Drawn on by the breeze

His unanswered whispers
Is anybody there?
Does anybody care?

As the silence descends
He's a soul with no friends.

When the moon has come up
And the sun has gone to bed
Everybody but one
Has gone to rest their head.

Hannah Stevens (10)
Woodley Junior School

My Dream Land

My dream land is made of cloud,
Nobody there talks too loud,
I like to go there in my sleep,
Everyone there earns their keep,
Nobody there wears dull clothes,
Everyone likes to strike a pose.

Everything there is made of sweets,
People like to meet and greet,
Everybody lives in a big mansion
And there's still room for an extension,
It is as big as a skyscraper
And they have posh toilet paper!

People in there are always mates
And they are never late,
There is no such thing as money
And it is always sunny,
You can hold love in your hand,
Yes, that would be my dream land.

Natalie Davies
Woodley Junior School

I've Got The Teacher Blues

I have got teacher blues,
Oh please don't send me to school,
I have got teacher blues
And I feel so ill,
Please don't send me to school,
I have got teacher blues
And all the kids will laugh at me,
As I have got the teacher blues.
Oh please don't send me to school
I have got teacher blues.

You know what it's like when people make fun of you
And you know what it's like when people are nasty
And also you know what it is like when you've got the teacher blues,
Oh please don't send me to school,
I have got the teacher blues.

Jess Martin (9)
Woodley Junior School

Animals

Dogs, dogs playing in the sun
Dogs, dogs having lots of fun
Dogs, dogs running down the path
Dogs, dogs they don't all like having a bath!

Cats, cats running in the house
Cats, cats chasing after a mouse
Cats, cats trying to catch a ball
Cats, cats climbing on the wall.

Birds, birds flying in the sky
They're enjoying themselves being up so high
Birds, birds with rainbow feathers
Birds, outside in all weathers.

Anon
Woodley Junior School

Dogs

Joe loved dogs he had a thousand at least,
From tiny lickers to great hairy beasts.
A gang of them would lick him all of the time,
While once was having a fine cherry wine.

He'd trained his dogs to do crafty tricks,
They'd jump on the postman and chase him with sticks.
You'd see them playing football in the park,
At half-time they would feast on a lark.

Joe was thrilled with his dogs' success,
While other people were calling them pests,
He gave them fresh orders but they said with a sneer,
'You're history, now dogs give orders around here!'

They threw Joe out he had five minutes to pack,
He left the house shouting, 'Just wait I'll be back.'
But they were too busy planning a plan,
To spread the world and take over from man.

Joe Brennan
Woodley Junior School

A Dog In The Street

A dog in the street,
That got beat in every dog race,
A man came along and took the dog home
And left it alone in the house.

An hour later the man threw the dog out,
The dog walked about the streets,
Past the alley cats and under a car,
Got out and got stuck in wet tar.

The owner followed the smell of mint,
And found some tar footprints
And heard a sound like a dog,
The owner found the dog on a log.

Ryan Morten (9)
Woodley Junior School

A Witch's Castle

In the witch's castle
Weird things happen in there
I once saw a horse having a battle
With the pig who likes to stare
Again I saw something wrong
Nothing to do with a horse
A bear singing a song
And a chimpanzee
Having a seven meal course

The witch came along
The bear stopped singing a song
The chimpanzee was full up
I dared not look
I ran home as fast as I could
I ran and ran and ran
I ran into my bedroom
And saw Mum flying up the stairs
On a brooooom.

Charlotte Cleary (9)
Woodley Junior School

Mates

Mates are funny, mates are cool,
cos they go to my school

They help me and I help them,
so don't blame me and don't blame them.

Me and my mates hang around,
on the streets playin' a funky sound.

We beat up boys
and make a lot of noise!

Me and my mates are really cool!

Daisy Roe (10)
Woodley Junior School

Beastly Bear

One fine evening in the new house,
When everything was as quiet as a mouse,
I was awake reading my book,
When I thought I saw Captain Hook.
I turned around to see who was there
And on a shadow on my curtain
I saw a beastly bear.
I opened the curtain only to see,
That it was the shape of a tree.
Every night I had no nightmare,
But only the dream of a cute, little bear.
Other people would get a big scare,
But to be honest I don't really care.
People would say it was really scary,
But really it just looks fat and hairy.
When I go out and see the tree,
I laugh saying, 'Silly me.'

Sophie Drummond (10)
Woodley Junior School

My Baby Brother

My baby brother, he is called Joel
Already seven months old, says, 'Da-da.'

I was so happy when he was born
And he was a boy!
I could not wait to see him.

He is growing up fast, eats solid food
His favourites are milky buttons and jelly.

He laughs a lot, dances to his songs,
Claps his hands along to Incy Wincy Spider
And likes playing games.

Kieran Mach (10)
Woodley Junior School

Chicken McNugeed

The world of Chicken McNugeed
Is a very strange place indeed
Dogs have to do SATs
And rabbits wear baseball caps
Turkeys hop round in ninja suits
And goats give off really loud hoots
In the world of Chicken McNugeed

In the world of Chicken McNugeed
Tigers eat lots and lots of cheese
Made of seaweed and bumblebees
Birdies ride skateboards with Tony Hawk
And vegetarians eat plenty of pork
Donkeys work at KFC
And mice have really wide knees
In the world of Chicken McNugeed

In the world of Chicken McNugeed
Spiders eat burgers and fries
Monkeys swallow fish and pepperoni pies
In the world of Chicken McNugeed
Chicken Mc Chicken Mc Chicken
The world of Chicken McNugeed.

Thomas Almond (10)
Woodley Junior School

Holiday Rap

I think holidays are really cool,
The sun is hot and there's a swimming pool,
There is a slide
And you can hide,
From my mates that are really cool.

I think holidays always rule,
Holidays are better than my school,
I think holidays are really fun,
I hate it when they're nearly done.

I love holidays and in my mind,
That will never ever change,
I'll keep looking forward 'til the next holiday comes,
That will never ever change.

Cameron Meadwell (9)
Woodley Junior School